I0531210

The Dasa's Guide to Sacred Gynarchy

How to Serve a Living Goddess
Viola Voltairine

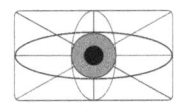

Artvamp Books

Copyright © 2026 by Viola Voltairine

Published by Artvamp Books

All rights reserved. No part of this publication may be reproduced, distributed, or transmitted in any form or by any means, including photocopying, recording, or other electronic or mechanical methods, without the prior written permission of the publisher, except in the case of brief quotations embodied in critical reviews and certain other noncommercial uses permitted by copyright law.

The publisher has no responsibility for the persistency or accuracy of URLs for any external or third-party websites referred to in this book and does not guarantee that the content on such websites is or will remain accurate or appropriate.

Artvamp Books is a division of:
Artvamp, LLC
6525 Gunpark Dr.
Suite 370-106
Boulder, Colorado 80301

www.artvamp.com

ISBN 979-8-9890097-3-2 (paperback)
ISBN 979-8-9890097-4-9 (eBook)

First printed December 2025

Contents

*A heartfelt thanks
to the devoted servants who proofread,
including alyosha, brett, dean, goodrock, jez, and
knee2srv.*

PROLOGUE

The Greatest Gift

The feeling was overwhelming gratitude as he lowered himself before his Living Goddess.

He was completely at peace, and every cell in his body seemed to be vibrating at the same frequency, like a steady warm glow. He was both excited and still, burning bright and silent as if time itself slowed and he had the room to roam around inside it. If a lightning strike could amplify pleasure, break you into millions of tiny pieces, and then stop the world from spinning so your particles would float without gravity, that is what it felt like. Yet every analogy fell short.

He could still feel the floor beneath him. He lay flat on his belly, right arm outstretched to her feet. The cool solidness supporting his entire body was comforting and grounding. And having her foot an inch from his fingertips made such a thrill rise from below, through the skin of his hand, arm, head, chest, torso, and legs. The ecstasy tickled his bones and sinews, playing them like a percussive instrument with every heartbeat.

He had never felt closer to anyone. It was almost as if an invisible umbilical cord connected them, and no words were needed to feel her absolute presence within him and all around him.

The sandalwood scent in the air became both a flavor and an emotion of its own. He had never felt anything like this, but his brain would also not allow him to analyze it. It had to be pure experience, which he could only reflect on later.

Later, she would tell him that they had become one, that he was now an extension of her. She reminded him that he would no longer have control. He was now a surrendered man. He had chosen a life of submission and service to her, directed by her purpose and vision.

After some time, he discovered that tears had been streaming down his face, as the love and gratitude flooded through him. His mouth was open, and he panted. His chest felt expanded and wide. His entire body felt so porous that even his anus and the pores of his skin seemed to be relaxed and eagerly yawning to let in her essence.

There was nothing in the world more precious than this experience, and to think so many denied themselves. It spoke of the pointless insanity most people unknowingly live. He could never go back.

INTRODUCTION

Who is this book for?

In the underground rumblings of women-only spaces and seeping through to the surface on social media there seems to be a quietly creeping consensus. The patriarchy is collapsing under the weight of its own failings. And the collapse is not going to be pleasant. Women and those we care about will need a plan in place to remain safe. We need to begin sowing the seeds of Gynarchy now, before things get more chaotic, so that the world which emerges from the aftermath of social upheaval is one ruled entirely by feminine principles and values. Many independent groups are working on this plan, designing sustainable communities, rethinking governance, family, religion, and power, and writing grimoires. The Devi Dasa Sacred Gynarchy is one.

The Service of Mankind Church calls the future world 'Eden 2.' Matriarchy Times and others call it Matriarchy. Some Messianic Jews and Christians fear it as the Apocalypse. We call it Gynarchy.

As Gynarchists, we refer to the transitional time we now live in as "The Pivot" - the era in which we finally collectively swing away from male dominance. Men will be the ones struggling most to find their bearings as this swing toward women's power and authority gains momentum. Therefore, I have written this book for those who are seeking purpose and are ready for women to show them their new role in a new paradigm. These men were never all that happy with the old paradigm of patriarchy in the first place and have always loved women and trusted our ability to lead.

The Devi Dasa Sacred Gynarchy consists of *Sacred Gynarchists*, who are members of our church, a registered non-profit religious organization in the U.S. The church is led by women, with the *Living Goddess* as the Central religious figure in each individual *Hive* (unique communities within Sacred Gynarchy). Other leaders include *Oracles*, who are the women organizing and managing the Hives, typically in small collectives. Men who have committed themselves to serving women within the Hive are called *servitors*. And finally, there are the beloved *dasas*, the men who have devoted their lives to the worship, support and care of a particular Living Goddess. They provide the labor for the running of the Hive. They are Her inner circle.

The dasa plays a specific role within Sacred Gynarchy as illuminated in this book. Though the role is typically meant for men, and this book is written as if the reader is male, I can imagine some women and non-binary people enjoying it as well. If so, I welcome you, regardless of gender. To determine if this book is for you, you need to ask yourself some questions.

Do you seek purpose and wish you could devote yourself completely to a Woman with a vision and the spiritual passion and power to bring it to fruition? Do you want to be used well for the cause? Do you respect and adore Women? Do you long to worship a real Living Deity and not an abstract idea? Does it pique your interest to be part of a movement and a community that intends to smother the patriarchy until it lacks the oxygen to survive, and to walk away from an oppressive sky daddy without embracing total atheism? This book will lead you on your next steps in that direction.

What's Inside?

The Dasa's Guide to Sacred Gynarchy originally began as a loose collection of writings and instructions compiled specifically for the devotees of Devi Viola Strepsata Voltairine, the first Living Goddess of the Devi Dasa Sacred Gynarchy. Any existing, new, or aspiring dasa can follow this guide.

It may also be used as a template and adapted to fit the worship of other Living Goddesses within our church. Any Living Goddess may copy the contents or modify them as Her vision dictates. It represents the fundamental practices, philosophy, and expectations of anyone who takes on the role of dasa within our organization.

Each section below is followed by journal topics centered on the knowledge being shared. This provides an opportunity for reflection and better comprehension. There is evidence that rewriting key ideas in your own words and discussing your response to them makes them easier to remember and assimilate. Journaling is an important practice within the church.

THREE SECTIONS

The first section within is a Practicum - the basic instructions for how to behave, and what actions to take as a devoted dasa. Start practicing now in preparation for acceptance as a dasa.

In the second section of the book, you'll find reprints of our church's essential sacred texts, including the Devi Doctrine - our core philosophy - as well as Articles of Belief, Missions, Purpose, and our Ten Commandments. These are meant to be references you can return to again and again for inspiration and guidance.

And if you are just starting out, the final section of the book gives you a full glossary of terms, quizzes to test your readiness, and step-by-step instructions for joining the church and working your way toward the dasa role. If you follow the instructions well, you will be asked to devote your life to Her as one of the most beloved and trusted servants of Gynarchy.

PRACTICUM

If you wonder what living as a dasa entails, read about the basic definition, the effects on your life, the expectations, the protocols, and the rites. Become familiar with the dasa experience and imagine yourself in the role.

What is a Dasa?

Standing outside the temple dedicated to Shiva is the figure of a bull. This is Nandi, the animal companion or "vahana" of the god. He is seated with a pleasant look upon his face, and one hoof raised so he is ready for action as soon as he is needed. He will wait contentedly for thousands of years, patient but eager to be called into service by his deity. To simply be near divinity is enough for him. His loyalty, and his alert and peaceful presence, are lessons in what devotion means.

Dasas emulate Nandi's spirit to cultivate inner resilience, spiritual discipline, and humble, selfless service to the divine. In Sacred Gynarchy, a dasa is chosen to serve one Living Goddess, engulfed in his love for Her, awaiting any opportunity to please Her and to make her life easier and more pleasant. A Living Goddess is the physical embodiment of Devi, the animating life energy - The Mother of All. She is both fully human and fully divine. By being both, She is the bridge between.

Becoming a dasa is a matter of total cathexis. All of his life energy is focused on Her and attending to Her every need and desire. This is the only way he can experience ecstasy. It is through devotion that the dasa grows and blossoms spiritually. He learns to set aside his noisy ego and become an extension of the divine, carrying out Her will.

A dasa is an embodiment of bhakti - total devotion. When one centers something or someone outside the self, the grip of hopelessness, apathy, and suffering are loosened. Failures do not stick. Successes are dedicated to the Goddess. Devotion is the meaning and purpose of his life and gives him sustenance through all difficulties.

This relationship is spiritual, of course, but fully and materially embodied, not some spacey kind of transcendent escapism. It is also romantic, as he pours all of his love into the Goddess. It is sexual in that all of his pleasure is focused on and derived from service to the Goddess and enhancing Her pleasure. He gives up control of his own sexuality to be directed exclusively by Her. If She wants him chaste, he will be chaste. If She wants him worked up into an erotic frenzy he will surrender to the feeling and let Her direct the show.

He does nothing for himself alone, but in dedicating himself so, his life is enhanced with deep satisfaction. He experiences an opening of the heart that allows him to be generous and kind in his dealings with the world around him.

He will rise to Her expectations. He will increase his competence to meet Her needs. He will become impossible to shame, drinking in humiliation as a sweet tonic to help wash away all his ego's reactive programming.

In practice, he will see a need or desire of his Goddess and attend to it. He will anticipate Her requirements and ask questions about how best to serve Her. He will follow any command so long as it does not harm another. He will hand over his resources as needed - time, attention, effort, labor, and material wealth. Sometimes it will be tedious, but the delicious flavor of devotion overcomes the tedium. Sometimes his patience and resilience will be tested, and he will then be given the invaluable gift of increased patience and resilience to take with him throughout his entire life.

A dasa is a consensual slave (the literal translation of the Sanskrit word "dasa," though it means so much more). Dasa is his identity, and all his beneficial personal qualities and skills are put to work for Her.

Being a dasa requires perpetual introspection, and continuous work. There is no end to the path, no goal or final outcome. It is not a path to somewhere in particular. It's a path of the ongoing experience of refinement until he becomes better and better, polished smooth like a river stone. One day, at the point of death, he ceases to be and has worn away each day of his life in the bliss of self-less service.

They say that bhakti - devotion - is the quickest method of becoming one with the divine in this life. But remember that enlightenment is not a far-off goal to be reached. The journey is the achievement and the entire purpose, and like the spiral of time itself, it lasts for the entirety of your conscious existence.

A dasa is one enraptured in the continuous process of becoming more devoted, less ego centered, and more enlivened by his present state of blissful surrender day by day.

The dasa and Living Goddess relationship is difficult to compare to other relationships. He is not a partner, but he is definitely in love. And the Goddess loves him in return, but from a different perspective - like a mother might love a child or like a person might love their pet. But those are also not appropriate analogies because there may be a sexual and romantic component to the relationship, necessary for the directing and transfer of erotic energy by the Goddess. The Goddess is also a teacher and the dasa a student. And yet it is so much more than that.

This is why we use the word dasa - a spiritual slave. Because the dasa gives up control and authority over his life to the Living Goddess and trusts Her to guide and direct him in whatever way She sees fit for his continual spiritual refinement.

The guru-shishya relationship in Sanatana Dharma (a.k.a. Hinduism) is similar to this. But Living Goddess and dasa may go even deeper in terms of absolute intimacy. It is the one and only relationship that is totally integrated into all aspects of a dasa's life holistically, with no aspect being off limits. Nothing is compartmentalized. It's also intended to become an eternal bond, unbreakable even across distance and time.

The Results of Devotion

Intimacy

There is no relationship more intimate than that of the Living Goddess and Her beloved dasa. Intimacy is defined as the symbiosis of knowing another and being known by another. The intensity of focus on Her means there is no one he could know more deeply. And he will be attentive to the Living Goddess even at Her most human and most imperfect. The dasa is hungry to know every detail about his Goddess so he can understand all that pleases Her or displeases Her.

Conversely, he will never hide anything about himself - his failures, his fears, his past, the parts of him that need work. Because he will let go of fear and show his vulnerability with bald honesty. She will see parts of him visible to no one else. All shame and embarrassment will dissolve in the light of complete transparency. She will see him as he is, in the raw, all defenses down. He will then be able to accept criticism with gratitude rather than deflection or defensiveness. This is the best way to grow into emotional maturity and spiritual fullness.

Ego Release

Devotion prompts the dasa to act beyond personal desires, which strengthens virtues and promotes selfless action. No longer is he focused on himself to the point of paralysis. The anxiety of who to become is answered with certainty in who he is. He decenters the demands of ego which urge him to compete with others in a hierarchy. It opens him to becoming a helpful, empathetic human being who cares about others and offers real value to the world.

Overblown egos lead to tyranny, exploitation, and destruction. Releasing the ego facilitates more co-operation and collaboration in both one's personal life and in society. It leads to a greater sense of unity, and a more aware and enlivened consciousness.

Discipline

Engaging in regular devotional practices helps build a structured lifestyle, fostering discipline, self-control, and the development of healthy habits. When he surrenders control to his Goddess She becomes his higher power. He will want to be at his best and most clear headed to serve Her well, so he will let go of vices that do him harm. He will want to be pleasing to Her so he will take care of his health and hygiene. She will give him rituals that anchor his life in a day-to-day rhythm so that ennui and laziness get overwritten by the comfort of routine. She gives him a reason to get up every morning and work through any struggles and setbacks. She provides accountability - a tangible reason to stick with the habits and tasks that keep him at his optimal level of physical and mental strength, and clarity.

Depth of Feeling

One of the main goals of a dasa's devotional practices is to attain "rasa," which is sheer bliss as the result of connecting with the essence of the Divine. If you have ever been deeply in love, you understand that it makes you capable of things you never knew possible. There is a certain bravery in exploring just how deeply one can love. Simply expressing love in the form of doing rituals or a daily pledge expands the heart.

What does that mean? We tend to get caught up in our heads. We get stuck in survival mode, which keeps us concerned with the surface level of all things. "Do this to get that" - it is the transactional mindset we are forced to adopt to get our basic needs met. But we are not here just to survive and engage in robotic exchanges. We are here to experience life in the fullest way possible and engage with all of the varied expressions of our unique humanity.

Through opening the heart, you discover that survival is the natural outcome, not the focus. Love and devotion create connection, and connection creates opportunities to give and receive. Love turns labor and tedium into acts of pleasure and affection. Loving a Goddess fully and unconditionally exercises your ability to give love in general, and sets the stage for creating a loving, giving, meaningful community.

A New Masculinity

Gender, it seems, has distinct effects on material reality, and it is not going away anytime soon. In recent generations, many men have begun to feel expendable, unwanted, or even ashamed of their gender. Some are offended by the ways women have changed, and by the abrupt end to the entitlement to women's attention and energy that was once taken for granted. These shifts have prompted a re-examination of what masculinity means and how it can evolve.

Masculinity - qualities or attributes typically associated with men. It's a neutral concept that has been socially and politically loaded for thousands of years, and heavily gatekept by a certain type of man who is absolutely terrified of being viewed as feminine. It is this kind of man who has been the subject of discussions about toxic masculinity - the unfortunate psychological condition of a man who thinks the worst possible fate is being seen as anything resembling a woman. These are the weakest and most insecure of the bunch, who think they have the power to set the parameters for manhood. They don't.

Masculinity is not inherently toxic. And to give men hope for their spiritual, psychological and social evolution, we must ask ourselves what a real and lasting masculinity can look like. To do that, we must establish an evolved definition of a man with regard to both qualities and actions. What defines a man, and what does a man do?

The following is a Gynarchist definition of a good man - a man who exemplifies manhood within our community. And if this definition suits you, then you're in the right place. Of course, women can also take on these qualities and actions as well, but one cannot be a good man without them. Without at least aspiring to embody these prerequisites to manhood, he is still a child.

1. A man is useful - he finds value in using his body, mind, skills, and talents to better himself and the lives of others.

2. A man is competent - he would never want to half-ass things and be seen as an oaf, so he puts his best effort into every task.

3. A man is eager to serve - being self-centered and transactional is a burden to others, and a man wants to unburden those around him as a show of his moral strength.

4. A man is true to his word - he follows through on promises and commitments.

5. A man is honest - he values truth and knows that lies lead to unnecessary drama. He is brave enough to accept consequences for

his own failings rather than hide them.

6. A man is accountable - he does not blame others for his mistakes or play victim when things go wrong. He deals with the reality at hand, acknowledging his role in successes and failures. He cleans up his own messes, literally and figuratively. He apologizes and makes things right when he falters.

7. A man protects - he would never harm or disadvantage those with less power, or those smaller or weaker than himself. He would, for example, never hit a child. And if he sees someone being treated badly or unfairly, he will step in to help.

8. A man has self-control and emotional intelligence - he feels his emotions deeply, bravely facing them head on and never repressing them. However, he knows that managing his emotions is his job not to be outsourced to women, and he does not allow them to run wild and harm others or himself. He can be angry without becoming frightening to those around him or lashing out, for example. He never expects others to fix him, but he asks for help when he needs it.

9. A man listens to understand - he does not assume he is always right, because if he did, he may miss out on important knowledge and information. He does not take every opportunity to show off his debate skills, and instead he seeks to achieve a real understanding of those with whom he engages.

10. A man shows respect to women - Women are the portals of life energy and creativity. He does not suck them dry, nor does he try to trap them, oppress them, repress their power, or claim ownership. He does not ask women for free labor, push their boundaries, or trample consent in any way. He understands women have power over him, and he is humbled by it.

What a Man is Not

A man is not defined by superficial markers such as clothes, hair, body shape, or mannerisms. Men's styles are ever-changing, and none of these inconstant attributes negate manhood. There is no one correct way to express your gender. A man can paint his nails, wear his hair long, shave his body, put on make-up, and put on a skirt without losing his identity as a man. A man can be pretty, sensual, and receptive and still be masculine. Gay men, dandies, and peacocks have always been men (and they are distinct from trans women who wish to be socially recognized as women - an entirely different category).

Conversely, I am feminine without being extravagantly so. I don't wear a lot of make-up or high heels. I don't perform femininity in any blatant way; I just am it - plain faced in comfortable pants. At one point in time, I'd have been seen as gender nonconforming - a masculine woman. But I am not the least bit masculine and am not perceived as masculine by anyone I know. I am a natural, witchy, dark feminine: the siren, the seductress, the bog hag, the wild woman. I wonder if any of those archetypes would immediately come to mind as quintessentially feminine to the kinds of men who treat their own masculinity as cosplay.

In studying the general characteristics of masculinity, I have also noted that men are not natural leaders. They are in fact naturally obedient. From my experience, men enjoy being told what to do. They submit to authority more readily than women, whose tendencies are more rhizomatic. Look at the social structures built by men. They gravitate toward clear and ordered hierarchies. The military is a good example. Men like to know their rank in the hierarchy and from whom they take their orders. From ancient courts to current corporations, man-made structures depend on the majority of men being submissive and obedient to someone. Logically, this demonstrates that the majority of men do not lead, contrary to what many claim.

The Spiritual Aspects of Manhood

I always describe the divine masculine as the trellis to the Feminine's flowering vine. He provides a supportive structure. He is the builder who makes the woman's vision a reality. He takes action on the Feminine's desires and makes sure that the infrastructure is in place so that her visions and plans can be realized. He holds the Feminine, giving her a safe container and a feeling of security. In turn, he is able to benefit from her love, sensuality and powerful life energy. He supports without expectation of reward but simply hoping that he may sometimes have the privilege of standing closer to the source of creation. He offers himself up, fully surrendered, ready to sacrifice and serve, but he never forces himself on her. And in doing this, he gains a genuine sense of purpose and even self-worth. Because if he is needed or wanted by a woman, then he must have real divine value.

Historically, courtly love exemplified this dynamic: knights risked everything for their Queen, driven by longing and devotion. Their masculinity was not diminished by their service; rather, it was defined by it. All of a knight's actions, all the risks he took, and all the grand sacrifices he made were driven by his romantic longing for his Queen. She was his reason to live. If he let her down, his heart would break at disappointing her. No one can say knights were not men.

Who determines the ideal masculinity?

If anyone should decide what makes a man, shouldn't it be the women whom men strive to be accepted by? If gender is, in part, a performance, shouldn't the performance of that femme-phobic macho mentality be reserved for men who only love other men? This codified man's man mentality is exclusionary of women in every way. So, it should also exclude men who love and adore women. The contemporary gatekeepers of masculinity only instruct on how to be a man who is attractive to other men. The only ones they want to impress are each other. They are most certainly homosocial, even if not homosexual. They do not hold the patent on masculinity. They are an unfortunate subset who work from a baseline anxiety about their own identity and worth. And their authority to write the rules of masculinity is illegitimate and imaginary.

Men have been the privileged class for so long that having them surrender and serve feels like justice and a realignment with nature herself. It feels as if the world is as it should be, and as it was before men pulled a trick of the mind (through religion and the hoarding of resources) to convince women to submit.

Gender and Sex

One thing I know for certain is that there is something very particular about being both female (sex) and a woman (gender). Our ovaries contain the mitochondrial DNA of human generations stretching back to the beginning of time. Mitochondria are the physical location of Devi (the Divine Feminine) within the body. They are the power source of living cells, and the locus of the animating force of life itself. Male bodies do not have the ability to pass on the life force. Sperm lack the proteins necessary to replicate mtDNA. It is not the men's role to carry on the memory of the ancestors, nor their burden (depending upon how you view it). The female body is literally a portal between the material world and the raw potential of all creation, and it contains an unbroken lineage beginning with the earliest human life on this planet. A female baby is typically born with the life codes passed from her grandmothers down through her to her own potential daughters. It rests within her ovaries from day one. She is the vital link between history and the future.

We all began as female. Male bodies came later as a support for female bodies. They carry a handful of genetic material that will prevent us from being clones of one another. This enables Devi's desire for endless variety to blossom. As an added benefit, the existence of male bodies and sexual reproduction makes us more resistant to microbes and reduces the number of genetic abnormalities passed down to our children. To put it simply, maleness is a useful adaptation, despite the disadvantages men present - like their general tendencies towards violence, aggression, and conquest. It is unnatural selection, wherein men take on the authority of mate selection, that amplifies those detrimental disadvantages. Men who would have never otherwise been chosen to reproduce found a clever hack to change the course of human evolution through manipulation, coercion and force.

Our population has now reached a point where reproduction is more of an option than a necessity. It has grown from one billion in 1804 to over eight billion now, adding another billion humans to the population every twelve years. If we keep multiplying at that pace, we will eventually exhaust the earth's resources. It would be irrational to think otherwise. In short, not all of us should reproduce. When and if we do, it is the responsibility of those who create and grow life within our bodies to determine who gets to mate with us. Female sexual selection determines the future of our species and the planet.

Not Just a Vibe

When you remove reproduction from the gender equation, we are left with energetics, aesthetics, and social roles. Aesthetics and social roles are fickle and amorphous constructs. Energetics typically do not significantly change in nature. Along with a female body, the majority of cis women (while acknowledging the outliers and exceptions) are born with particular energetic capabilities and powers that would take men decades of intense study to vaguely emulate. Not coincidentally, a lot of spiritual paths, from meditation and yoga to qi gong, were designed by men for men with the aim of doing just that. Yes, I'm saying men's paths of self-improvement and spiritual evolution intentionally redirect them toward a more intimate understanding of the feminine. Though theoretically possible, changing your energetic make-up takes a whole lot of focused effort! Though the masculine cannot become fully feminine in energy, with discipline it can refine itself and become closer to divine and a perfect energetic complement to the feminine. A spiritually developed man loses the drive for ego-inflation and conquest, and he becomes more of an asset to his community than a source of conflict.

Women's innate energetic superpowers were one of the primary reasons men felt we had to be reined in by patriarchy. We were subjected to a destiny swap, trapped and held captive by men who need our energetic gifts to thrive. We are the vital creative resource to which men crave access, so men needed to invent a society wherein women would feel dependent on them. It was only through devising laws and social norms that steal women's agency and autonomy that men could produce the illusion of their own exaggerated relevance. Otherwise, we might treat them just as female bees treat drones–useful for mating but pushed away from women and community as an unnecessary drain on resources once their utility is finished. This is a primal fear hidden deep in the heterosexual male psyche, which is why they devote so much of their lives, even under patriarchy, to pursuing sustained access to women.

Energetics is an esoteric subject. But, put simply, even the most masculine-presenting women have unique energetic signatures that make them different from men. Gender as a social role, or an aesthetic expression, has little to do with this particular facet of the feminine and masculine. And indeed, even completely infertile women, and women missing a uterus or ovaries, are still a source of potent erotic life energy. This means that the ability to reproduce is not a prerequisite condition of this phenomenon.

What does this mean in relation to men? In short, a man who is pretty, dresses in sensual fabrics, accentuating his softer features, taking on a more receptive attitude is naturally as much a man as the more utilitarian, aggressive, rough and rugged man from an energetic standpoint. Social perception of manliness is a separate facet of manhood. He could walk into a room and be perceived as a pretty man. Or he could even be perceived as some in-between gender - a sissy, or androgynous. Even so, he still will not possess the energetic powers of the feminine, and he can still possess all the best qualities of the ideal masculine as outlined in my previous description. The refined man is most satisfied and fulfilled in his manhood when he strives to be an asset and a support to women rather than a predator or oppressor.

Before you brush this discussion of energetics off as far out woo woo, consider the phenomenon that food becomes flesh. Ponder for a moment the fact that proteins and carbohydrates each have distinctly different roles in the process of turning a sandwich into a human body. This too is an aspect of energetics. Our human experience is rooted in what can be referred to as alchemy. Our bodies are mechanisms for transmuting energy into form, sensation, thought, emotion and action. And in alchemy, specific formulas and conditions create particular results. The spiritual is the physical, and we are discussing the workings of material reality. From the alchemical perspective, it is easier for feminine energy to be broken down into masculine energy than for masculine energy to be refined to the point of transmuting into feminine energy. It's a bit like turning lead into gold. It can be done, but requires a light speed induced nuclear reaction. Perhaps this analogy helps to illustrate the motivation behind men's project of entrapping and enslaving women over the past five to ten thousand years. They long to conquer and own what they cannot, without almost godly effort, become.

And before you accuse me of biological essentialism, remember that physical sex characteristics are just one piece of the puzzle and that none of this is a clean binary. There are outliers, a small percentage

of humans, whose energy is neither entirely masculine nor feminine, but a third (or fourth or fifth)
type. These people are marginalized and oppressed
along with women in a patriarchal system because
they seem to defy the usual energetic limitations
and they throw a wrench into the patriarchal power
project. Perhaps they themselves are the philosopher's stone in human form, and that is why some
cultures give them a special place as healers or
sages.

Here I must insert a somewhat controversial view
- that there is a definite difference between a man
who cosplays as a woman, taking on superficial feminine characteristics, and a genuine trans woman.
And if our culturally constructed gender norms
were not so heavily codified, some who identify as
trans might no longer feel the need to do so. Trans
women identify as women in a way that elevates the
concept of woman as powerful and central. They
were assumed to be men, but they never were. They
are willing to accept the disadvantages of being both
a woman and trans within a misogynistic patriarchal society in order to simply be true to who they
are. They must be protected from the oppression of
patriarchy even more than cis women in some cases, because they subvert and delegitimize the patriarchal gender hierarchies. Energetically aligned
trans women (as opposed those who simply adopt
the social, cultural, and aesthetic markers) make
up less than one percent of the population. They
are rare and, even when perceived by others as
female, they are energetically distinct from both
cis women and cis men. It's interesting to witness
how contemporary Western culture struggles with

this concept much more than many other cultures have in the past. Those like the Hijra of India and so-called two-spirit people of various indigenous North American peoples have been an acknowledged phenomenon for a very long time. It just further illuminates the stranglehold patriarchy has on white Western society.

It is becoming more common for the energetic outliers to fully embrace their non-binary nature, feeling that conforming to the constructs of either man or woman is disingenuous. Also, as I have inferred, there are also feminine humans who successfully engage in the simpler transmutation of feminine energy into masculine to live as trans men. Feminine energy, being the basis of life itself, can be reshaped in new ways. The interplay between energetics, the body, identity, and social signalling results in a myriad of distinct possibilities, a bit like gender recipes, or constellations. Even contemporary westernized gender theorists, though well meaning, may sometimes obfuscate matters because of the aftereffects of misogyny and the struggle to free themselves from the grip of its pre-programmed gender norms. For political reasons, some may view gender as nothing more than a declaration of identity, and claim that the only prerequisite for embodying a specific gender is to make a statement to that effect. That approach diminishes the significant and complex experience of gender to an almost insulting degree. It is clearly more than just a label to claim at will.

TERFs - trans exclusionary radical feminists - are simply a reactionary byproduct of patriarchy and its envious mockery of the feminine. I feel they are reacting to the feminine cosplayers I mentioned before. However, in my view, those who are feminine-presenting are mostly just harmless gender rebels and definitely not deserving of the loathing heaped upon them by this subgroup of women. I feel a lot of misplaced anger in their rhetoric, turning their rage and frustration with misogyny against the marginalized. And they often seem blind to the exceptions to the binary that can and do exist. Given my explanation of congenital gendered energetics, I anticipate that some stubbornly pedantic readers might want to lump me in with TERFs. But in fact, I have spent many hours arguing against their hateful rhetoric, and criticizing their alliance with religious fundamentalism. A lot of their concerns revolve around women-only spaces. I say that if all spaces become women's spaces – safe and comfortable places where women can exist without being intruded upon, objectified, threatened, or assaulted – then we would no longer need spaces that exclude anyone. That is a worthwhile project we should work on, not drawing lines to further marginalize a small minority of people.

Affirming Gender

As I have already made clear, I have absolutely no problem with the variety of ways in which people express gender. And whether one is a trans woman from an energetic standpoint, or simply actively embodying the social and aesthetic characteristics of what our culture labels feminine, I never condone hate or discrimination, and I happily accept people as they are without debate, so long as they are not clownishly mocking the feminine. I am only explaining the different layers that make up what we call gender and how they may play into our evolved and unbound concept of masculinity. Keep in mind that we all start out as female in the womb. Just as there is a biological transformation that creates the male sex before birth (as well a few other rare sexes besides male or female), there is an energetic trans-mutation of feminine life energy into the masculine, and even a social and cultural process of "becoming a man."

I know there are those who want gender to be a simple binary based on sex organs and gametes, neatly matched up to social expectations and ap-pearances. It makes things easier. But they don't realize that this forces everyone around them to conform in order to make *them* feel secure in their gender. Cisgender folks engage in gender-affirming care constantly because being accepted and vali-dated as their gender feels good. The common fact that there are men's and women's clothing sections in department stores is one glaring example. A man being told he's a real man gives him a self-esteem boost (and this is as true for both trans men and cis men).

Gender can be a slippery concept, sometimes diffi-cult to pin down. When you realize that it encom-passes so many different layers of meaning, from the spiritual to the physical and from superficial markers to energetic signatures, I can't blame some people for wanting to do away with the concept of gender altogether. However, I not only find that im-possible, I would also abhor a world without it. I am attached to my womanhood in every way. And I have a powerful turn-on regarding being a woman to whom men submit. To be a woman worshipped and obeyed by men feels rich in historical, social, and spiritual significance, and is psychologically pleasing beyond compare. Affirming my woman-ness in contrast to your man-ness contributes to my overall life satisfaction. I would dislike an androgynous world. It would feel like a culturally imposed lie forced on me in order to satisfy a handful of people who can simply opt out on a personal level instead of compelling others to conformity. The lack of erotic tension and power play between genders and sexes would bore me to tears.

Expression of Gynarchic Masculinity

The masculinity embraced with Gynarchy can be rugged and tough, but it is also secure enough to be soft, sensual, gentle, and pretty without fear. It is not solely attached to a specific aesthetic expression or a macho code of conduct. It's a masculinity that adores and serves the Feminine without any shame, and can even define itself in relation to that role. It cannot be held hostage by the anxious and insecure men who think they own it. It is a courageous masculinity that busts through the bounds it was imprisoned within from birth. It will not be strangled with fretting over its own validity nor work to appease other men who seek to control it.

Just as male birds naturally perform their masculinity to please female birds, I think masculinity can find a variety of creative ways to show itself that are not constricted by homosocial preferences. Men in other cultures and in different eras have not adhered to the strictly policed expression contemporary Western men are expected to embrace. We know that real and securely held masculinity is not meant to be tied down to being angular, plain, and utilitarian. There's also nothing wrong with utilitarian expression - I like to wear comfortable clothing myself. But it need not be coded as exclusively masculine, nor the primary expression of masculinity.

As a general rule of thumb, just be mindful of your motives. Genuine self-expression should be the goal, over contrived performance. Mockery of the feminine or viewing qualities that are socially seen as more feminine as a form of sexual humiliation points to a covert form of misogyny that needs to be examined and deconstructed. Ask yourself what is inherently shameful about wearing lacy panties or painting your nails, for example. When you are no longer trapped in a patriarchal mindset, the only truthful answer is absolutely nothing.

Ignore the voices that build walls around manhood to keep you out and be as you are. Embrace the qualities and actions of a good adult man that I outlined above and otherwise express your gender in any way that feels good to you.

For me, the thrill of a good man who submits to and serves women, regardless of how he expresses or displays himself, is so delicious. It feels like the natural order of things. It feels like righting all the wrongs of history. It gives me a sense of euphoria as a woman to have men at my feet. It breaks the nightmare spell of misogyny. It's powerful magic that I am unwilling to give up.

Body and Sexuality in Sacred Gynarchy

In Sacred Gynarchy, we believe body is spirit, body is soul. We do not make any distinction because we know that all matter is the vibration of Devi Herself. Even inert objects are made of vibration. Without vibration, nothing can exist. Our bodies are made of Her vibration (a reality understood by ancient rishis and contemporary scientists alike), and that vibration creates everything we can experience with our five senses and even beyond our five senses. Every thought, every feeling, every sensation, every movement and shape are the stuff of Devi. Unlike in other religions, the body is never seen as a separate or debased part of the whole. Detachment from and denial of the body are sacrilegious attempts to deny reality. This is the opposite of materialism, that says matter is all. There is no physical and spiritual division. This is a doctrine of non-duality, with no hierarchy. The physical is the emotional, is the mental, is the spiritual - all are the energy of vibration (which can also be thought of as consciousness). Mind over matter is not mind working against matter but recognizing that the two are the same and that changing one simultaneously changes the other.

This informs our approach to sex and eroticism. The erotic is the ultimate expression of creative life energy. We celebrate it and we celebrate female pleasure and the female orgasm. We delight in sex beyond penetration because only eighteen percent of women can orgasm through penetration alone. A turned-on woman is a powerful woman and a powerful leader and guide. She is lit from within. When used by women, erotic energy can reduce pain, can heal wounds faster, and can clarify the mind and reveal the right path in terms of decision-making.

It is critical that women have full control of all sexual experiences, deciding when, where, how and with whom sex happens. We believe that women require absolute control over their own bodies and should have the freedom to have any kind of sexual encounters they wish, whenever they wish. Women must definitely decide which men deserve access to heterosexual sex and which men should go without for their entire lives. No, not all men deserve sex, and we know this. We gatekeep pussy, as well we should. And we decide which men get to pass on their genes. These decisions were made our sole responsibility by Devi and nature itself.

Conversely, we teach men to harness erotic energy through orgasm denial and semen retention, sometimes using chastity as an aid on the path. The female body brings erotic energy straight from the center of the earth, holding it at our core. The more we feel, the more we can draw into ourselves and bring out into the world. The male body must borrow energy from the female body, first from their mothers, and later from partners and the women around them. Watch carefully, and you will notice how often women in social settings are feeding life energy into men. Once you witness it, you can't unsee it.

This natural flow of energy from women is not a bad thing, but for millennia, men have used women as erotic batteries. It is why men have pursued women and often seem obsessed with sex. Even gay men absorb erotic life energy from women. Men require training to be able to recycle and regenerate erotic energy and give back to women. Otherwise, they run the risk of draining us, and many women do not know how to keep up with regenerating what is taken from them. They become depleted. This is why there is often a mismatch of libidos within marriage. Women have been sucked dry, and men release what they gain through too frequent orgasms and then need more and more from women.

Men must stop releasing life energy through their orgasms, causing themselves only to need to absorb more from the women in their vicinity. And women must learn to consciously stop leaking life energy when they do not intend to give it away. Women must expand their capacity to hold energy in their bodies. Men must learn to recycle it within themselves, keeping some on reserve, and learning to give some back to women when needed.

With orgasm denial and semen retention, men will discover that they feel more energized, more focused, and less likely to do harm or draw more from women than necessary. They also experience a deeper level of devotion. In a state of prolonged arousal without release, a man's psyche is reshaped toward selfless service and adoration. He is able to fully experience the erotic effects of women, and the erotic life energy at its peak.

Our emphasis on male denial is not based on taboos against sex or some kind of purity culture. On the contrary, we understand the intense power of the erotic and understand how it should be wielded by women with complete and utter sexual control and freedom.

And one last note: The fact that women decide when, how, and with whom to have sex does not mean a woman can force or coerce a man to have sex with her when he is resistant or hesitant to do so. Remember, bodily autonomy is one of the Pillars of Gynarchy. Consent is always respected and required for any kind of activity, including sexual activities. Rape, whether committed by men or women, is as wrong as murder.

General Expectations

Being the dasa of a Living Goddess is a bit like living as a monk. It is a careful and persistent chiseling of your own character into a refined and strengthened servant to the Divine Feminine. You'll wear away all that is reactive and unnecessary and be left with a more authentic version of your own personality. In doing so you will find your spiritual, emotional, physical and intellectual development and your well-being arrive as beneficial side effects. This creates more ease and less struggle in your life.

To be a dasa is to be someone that can be relied upon by his Goddess and who is a needed and valued part of his community. It is neither an extremely difficult life nor is it a lazy one. It may be a challenge to throw off your old ego-centered ways, but your Living Goddess will be there to guide you and remind you of your purpose. And once you fully surrender, you will find yourself moving like water, flowing around the obstacles in your life with very little friction.

Below are some of the general expectations of you as a dasa. Read and discover where you might find resistance. Examine that resistance when it arises and ask yourself what you are protecting. Is there a vulnerability you are guarding and why? Sometimes it only takes a shift in perspective to overcome that resistance.

Devotion - You will bow to your Goddess in reverence no matter your mood. There is not one wish or desire of your Goddess that you will not do everything in your power to fulfill. If She expresses that She needs or wants an action from you, you will hear it and respond with effort to bring Her joy, for Her pleasure and safety are your life purpose.

Obedience - Find clarity and life's meaning in your Goddess's command and resist only that which may cause serious harm to yourself and others. Develop trust through experience - note examples of Her trustworthiness as a way to strengthen your faith in Her leadership.

Chastity - As a dasa, your pleasure is no longer yours to control, but the domain of women only. You will not find sexual indulgence nor release without the express permission or behest of a lady, be She Goddess, Oracle, Queen, or Mistress. And at the request of the lady who has authority over you, you will give Her pleasure in the ways She prefers until She has Her fill.

Self-respect - You will understand yourself and hold strong to the personal boundaries which, if crossed, will cause you serious distress or personal harm. It is your responsibility to communicate these boundaries clearly and without hesitation or shame. If your Goddess cares for you, She will take them seriously.

Cleanliness - Both body and surroundings must be kept clean, neat, and in good repair. This is a matter of daily persistence. Create automatic habits and rituals that will make this task easier. Never make anyone else clean up after you, and clean up after others whenever you see any opportunity. Never think, "it is not my responsibility." All jobs are your jobs, which you should feel eager to complete. What an embarrassment to leave for others something you could have easily done yourself. Take pleasure in your hygiene routines as well - in bathing and polishing your teeth and trimming your hair. Being pleasant to the senses should be your standard for both your body and surroundings. You should allow yourself to feel pride in a space and mind free of dirt and clutter.

Resilience - See every failure or fuck up as an opportunity to learn and improve and waste zero time in self-pity. Apologize for any mistake or misstep and correct it. Energy wasted on self-flagellation is energy that could be better used on improving yourself or helping others. Wallowing is counter-productive. Do not turn anger at your failures in on yourself because no one can improve himself by ripping himself to shreds. If there is a consequence for your failure, allow your Goddess to decide it, for that is Her responsibility, not yours. Discipline can only be gained by repeatedly facing failure and moving past it. It is a necessary part of the process.

Selflessness - All you do from now on is for the good of Goddess and Hive. Never think of reward or transaction, only serving. For you, life's meaning and your pleasure is found in service and devotion.

Remember that even efforts made toward your own health and wellbeing (exercise, rest) are done so that you may be in the optimal shape to serve others well.

Wellness - You will live in such a way that you optimize your own vigor and physical and neurological wellness. For an unhealthy dasa cannot function at his best for his Goddess. You will eat clean, nutritious food, sleep regularly, hydrate well, meditate, and always work to improve your flexibility, balance, and endurance. Present your body as a gift to your Goddess, crafted with intention and care.

Persistence - Show up every day and do your best on that day. When you take the focus off your own ego, it becomes easier to show up and make some effort or progress. There will be days when you are bored. Do something to make your tasks more fun - add an element of play or gamify your experience. Keep records of your efforts and see if you can compete with yourself to improve in some way. If you are too exhausted or feeling ill, then rest, recover, and come back refreshed to start again. But be mindful that momentum is easier to maintain than to restart.

Competence - There is nothing more disrespectful and insulting to your Goddess than half-assing a task before you. It shows disdain for your Goddess and Hive. Always be present and focused on the task at hand and do it to the best of your ability. You may find you need more knowledge to complete the task. In which case, educate yourself or find someone who knows more than you to help. And never use your own incompetence as a tactic to wiggle out of a duty given to you. Every difficult project is an opportunity to learn and improve yourself. Do not shy away from a challenge.

Graciousness - Accept being asked to serve as a privilege and avoid complaining. Complaining lets the woman or Goddess you serve know that She is a bother to you, and you have more important ways to spend your time and efforts. Is that kind of disregard the feeling you wish to convey? Also, live as if you are nearly impossible to offend. If the words of another hurt you, you will feel the sting. However, you must practice consciously releasing the pain and becoming curious about why the other person may be acting out. Perhaps you can respond in a way that creates more peace in the environment. Learn to acknowledge and feel your emotions fully and then find ways to regulate before reacting (remove yourself from a tense situation if necessary, and weep, rage, or vent, and then return with a clear he ad).

Minimalism - A dasa lives simply and, most importantly, takes up very little space. You should have no more private belongings than can fit into a large footlocker (or at most a small van if you live alone). This includes clothing, shoes, toiletries, leisure items such as games, books, technology, collectibles, and other highly personal items. All else should be shared property with the Hive. If you whittle down your private belongings to only those that benefit your life in a real way, you will find you've been hanging on to a lot that you do not need. Other personal things that can be shared, such as furnishings, appliances, and the like, should be shared so that they can benefit the greatest number of people.

Intelligence - Refining yourself to be the best, most obedient dasa you can be does not mean having no critical thinking skills or no deep interests in other topics. Continue to pursue your curiosity and work on being more aware of the world of the past and present, as well as potentials for the future. Do not stop asking questions. Devotion and obedience are not mindless, and your competence is only enhanced by the pursuit of knowledge. In your humility, you understand that there is always more to learn.

Non-comparison - Stop yourself before comparing your efforts or abilities to another, including your Goddess. We all begin at different stages, and all will make steps toward being wiser and more competent at a different pace. Compete only with yourself at your current best, and never with those outside yourself. Give grace to yourself and others during low points.

Remember that your process of self-improvement is never done. Do not think there is an achievable end goal or the possibility of ultimate perfection. The process is the whole point of the practice, and it is a lifelong on-going process. If you are continuing to grow and refine yourself, it will never become effortless. However, the more you practice focusing on the cultivation of these desired attributes, the more you will grow strong and flexible enough to handle bigger challenges with grace, which will lend more ease to your life and more gratifying interactions and relationships with others.

In an effort to clarify the expectations for my own dasas, I formally codified them and distributed them to those devoted to me as their Living Goddess.

THE DASA CODE

Before accepting the role of personal dasa to Viola Devi, you must understand and agree to the following:

- You will be honest. Viola Devi will not tolerate lies or withholding relevant information about yourself or your activities past or present. This is the number one deal breaker. Even when truth is hurtful or inconvenient, it is preferred over lies and secrets. Admit your faults and mistakes quickly, even if you feel shame.

- You will be loyal. Viola Devi may engage physically, emotionally, or romantically with whomever she pleases, when and wherever she pleases, and however she pleases, while keeping your safety and well-being in mind. However, you will need Viola Devi's approval before engaging with others. She may direct you to serve others, and you are allowed to refuse. However, if you wish to engage with someone not presented to you by Viola Devi you must obtain express permission beforehand. As a dasa of Viola Devi, you understand that this is not a partnership of equals.

- You will take care of yourself. You belong to Viola Devi, and you will take good care of what is Hers. Self-inflicted damage is never allowed. You will eat in a way that nourishes your body, and take supplements as needed. You will get adequate sleep, you will drink plenty of water, and you will attend to your physical and dental health with regular maintenance and check-ups. You will not take unreasonable risks which could lead to injury or worse. You will pay attention to your hygiene and skincare. You will get regular exercise and do stretching and yoga to maintain flexibility and prevent chronic physical ailments. You will practice methods of stress control and relief such as meditation and breathwork. In short, you will treat your body as a valuable possession of the Goddess to be maintained to the highest standard. To do otherwise is grave insult to Her.

- You will cultivate emotional intelligence. You will identify emotions and express them in productive ways. You will learn non-violent communication. You will not repress emotions, positive or negative, but instead feel them fully, process and alchemize them. You will do shadow work to discover the unconscious parts of yourself that are in the way of healthy emotional regulation. You will seek help in times when you are stuck, or life is difficult due to mental health issues. You will give yourself grace when you struggle.

- You will love yourself. Self-loathing and self-deprecation are just as egocentric as self-aggrandizement and not allowed. Negative self-talk should be headed off immediately. You will identify and correct these patterns. If you are loved by the Goddess, then it is an insult to Her if you treat yourself as worthless. Self-insult is a clear statement that you think the Goddess is stupid and wrong for loving you.

- You will be as consistent as humanly possible. There will be times when you falter at following through with what is expected or desired of you. The key is to move forward and continue with your practices and good habits even after you drop the ball. Just pick it up again where you left off and show by your efforts that the Goddess is your priority. Consistency and persistence show your genuine and abiding love for the Goddess.

- You will prioritize Viola Devi. You will show your love for the Goddess by making her desires and needs your top priority over everything else, including work, hobbies, friends, and family. You will find Viola Devi is very understanding when other things arise that need your attention if you have shown in all other ways that she is your primary concern.

- You will listen and follow directions. Pay attention. If Viola Devi gives a specific instruction, it is significant and should be followed as given. Ask for clarification if you are unsure. Don't pretend you have heard and understood when you have not. By default, do

NOT take the details of her commands as mere suggestions, but as law. If you have suggestions for better ways of doing things, check in before making any changes.

- You will share your inner life with your Goddess. Withhold nothing of yourself from Viola Devi, even if it is embarrassing, scary, or humiliating. Expose all things. Allow your Goddess total intimacy.

- You will continually learn new things to improve the life of Viola Devi and the Hive. Teach yourself new skills, read books, take classes, and continually advance your skills and knowledge.

- You will abandon transactional thinking and serve selflessly. Serving is an honor, and you will find yourself much more satisfied mentally and emotionally if you serve without any expectations. Your labors and resources given to another instantly double in their value. To expect reward or recognition is ego-driven.

- You will leave every space better than you found it. If everyone does this, no one will have extra work to do. Tidy up, make small repairs as needed, organize, and beautify every space you enter before you leave, and you will be a gift and benefit to everyone else. It is never "not my job." Clean up after yourself and others without complaint, and you will maintain a pleasant environment.

- You will see the work, do the work, and stay out of the misery. Complaining and moaning about work to be done is a fruitless waste of energy and sucks away the energy of Goddess and others. Use that energy instead to accomplish the task at hand. If you have taken on more work than you can handle, discuss it rationally like an adult and don't whine.

- You will take up less space. Be aware of the space you take up and be considerate of others. This may mean keeping the number of objects you own to a minimum, allowing others room on a bench or at a table. Sprawling, both with your body and your belongings is a form of entitlement and marking your territory. Avoid such patriarchal behavior. Simplify your life. You should own no more private belongings than absolutely necessary. All else should be shared communally.

- You will have interests. There will be moments when your time and attention are not needed or desired. When not serving the Goddess, you will have plenty of other interests that keep you busy, enhance your enjoyment of life, and make you a more interesting human.

- You will help those in need. When possible, find ways to be helpful to those who have less than you or who are experiencing suffering. Make yourself useful in every context possible. Never turn away from genuine need. Step in if someone is in trouble.

- You will strive to quiet the ego. Maintain only enough ego to allow yourself to understand your individual and unique presence in the world - just enough to keep yourself from becoming untethered from your day-to-day reality. Be aware when the ego becomes too demanding or defensive and strive to recognize the difference between ego and intuition.

- You will strive to recognize intuition. Take note when you have a hunch that turns out to be correct or when it is wrong and turns out to be fear or paranoia. Start to learn what strong intuition feels like until you can tell when your gut feelings are important. Learn how fear and anxiety feel in contrast.

These expectations are not negotiable.

V.1.1 Created: September 19, 2025

Dasa Protocols

BASIC

Basic protocols are non-negotiable requirements for all dasas.

The Pledge

To be spoken aloud in person or sent to Viola Devi as an audio or video message at least once per day.

I **accept** the natural authority of women.
I **submit** to the authority of Viola Devi.
I **affirm** that this is what I truly want:
To **worship** and **obey** Viola Devi.
To **devote** myself to you - body, mind, and soul.

I **respect** and **love** you, divine Goddess,□
And unconditionally trust your ability to lead me.
I **surrender** my ego
and **defer** to your better judgement.
My purpose is to **support**, **serve**, and **please** you.
I **accept punishment** for any infraction.
I will **sacrifice** my needs and follow your will.

Only if you are ready and willing to do so with honest sincerity, you may add the following lines to make this a 108-word pledge.

Your say is final.
I hold no others above you.
You own me.
My life is yours to control.

The Journal

To be written daily. This is an essential method of communication to the Living Goddess as well as an excellent tool for self-reflection and inner growth.

In Viola Devi's Hive, they are saved to Google Docs every day, and shared to her gmail account.

You may write freestyle about anything you wish but when you get stuck, use one or more of the following prompts:

1. How did you serve selflessly today?

2. How did you leave a space better than you found it?

3. In what way did you honor the Feminine?

4. Log your obedience practices for the day and any emotions or sensations related to those.

5. If you meditated, did you notice any differences in your body after or have any insights?

6. Write about things in your personal history that you want to share with Devi.

7. Write about events in your day that you want to share with Devi.

8. What are some things about yourself you are embarrassed or hesitant to share?

9. Did you gain any insight from a discussion online or a Satsang?

10. Can you discern between ego and intuition? Give an example.

11. Are there any mental health issues you have struggled with? How have you tried to address them? Are you able to tolerate uncomfortable emotions?

12. Envision your future as part of the Hive if you plan to join us. What does it look like? What is your everyday life like while there?

13. What most concerns you about your present? What most excites or delights you about your present?

14. What most concerns you about the future? What most excites and delights you about the future?

15. How good are you willing to have this world? How far are you willing to go to fulfill your destiny?

16. Are you abstaining from orgasm? For how long? How is that journey going? What have been your biggest hurdles? What new insight have you gained?

17. When in a place where you feel stuck, upset, agitated, and down do you know how to accept and alchemize those feelings? Are you able to create a state change that

helps move the emotion through you? If so, how (dance/movement, walking/running, rest/sleep, chanting/singing/screaming, cold shower/dip, etc.)? Describe your process of dealing with your own dark feelings.

18. Do some creative writing: fiction or poetry.

Check-in

Your Living Goddess will require a daily check-in or a simple greeting each morning. In our Hive, dasas greet Viola Devi and the other dasas each day in the dedicated Discord server (an app used for chatting via text, audio and video) in the #good-morning channel. Then they share something in one or more of the other channels that may be of interest to the Hive. This can be a thought, a recommendation, a photo, a meme, music, a video, an article, etc. They are expected to respond to each other's posts to keep the server active and foster community.

INTERMEDIATE

Intermediate and advanced protocols are ways to express, enhance, and advance your devotion.

Puja

Bowing to your Living Goddess every day is a spiritual practice that puts you in the right mindset. If you are unable to do this in person, set up your camera and take a pic of yourself bowing to your Living Goddess, facing her general direction geographically. Do this in the turtle position, on your knees, right arm extended, forehead on the floor or ground, left arm tucked under your body, palms down. Make yourself as low to the ground as you are physically able to manage (Don't worry if you are not very flexible at first, as repeating this daily will help with flexibility. Just do the best you are able in your current condition.). See the image here for proper form. It is preferred that you do so in the nude if possible and, if your Goddess has gifted you a collar or symbol of your Seva of some kind, wear that in the photo. In our Hive, this is posted to the #puja channel on the Discord server every day. Feel free to get creative with the images if the mood strikes. Some of our dasas make an art of it.

If you are able, you may also deliver or send a small bouquet for the altar on the new moon and/or full moon. Red or dark purple flowers are best for a new moon, and white flowers represent the light of the full moon. Choose flowers that will last more than one week and have a sweet scent. Small potted flowers are also acceptable.

Another option is to deliver or send silver or gold pieces (coins, rounds, bars, or jewelry made of pure gold or silver or other precious metals). These will be consecrated on the altar, then saved to fund the Temple and its activities.

And finally, you may also deliver or send specific sweets requested by your Living Goddess to be consecrated on the altar. This is often referred to as "Prasad." Viola Devi asks for ceremonial grade cacao that is ethically sourced, and which will be consumed in cacao ceremonies guided by Her.

You are encouraged to keep a personal altar in your living space if possible (it is not required, but it helps you to maintain a sense of connection). The altar should include:

- *an image of your Living Goddess*

- *a symbol of the divine feminine of your choosing (a Goddess or yoni figure or image, or any representation that evokes the feeling of divinity for you)*

- *a symbol of your surrender and submission (this can be very personal - a whip, a collar, a binding of some kind, etc.)*

- *and a lamp (oil diya) or candle to be lit during puja and/or meditation*

Optionally, you may also offer fresh flowers (they can be wildflowers from around your home or neighborhood) on your personal altar weekly or on new and full moons. Make sure they are always fresh, and if they do not already have a sweet scent, add a bit of sandalwood oil or paste to them for fragrance.

Other acceptable items: a small bowl of water or a shell filled with water, incense, printed quotes. If you have any consecrated items offered to you by your Living Goddess, you may keep these on the altar as well. Altars are intensely personal and should evoke in you a feeling of devotion and reverence. If you are Viola Devi's dasa, you should share occasional photos of your altar in the #puja channel on Discord as inspiration and a show of devotion.

Meditation

Use the personal mantra given to you by Viola Devi or your meditation teacher. Sit in a comfortable position. Close your eyes. For the first time, say it out loud many times, becoming quieter and quieter each time until it is repeated only silently and mentally. Each time you sit to meditate, close your eyes and repeat the mantra mentally over and over with your eyes closed for 21 minutes. There is no need to say it out loud after the first time.

If other thoughts come, or if you lose the mantra, just return to the repetition as soon as you notice. Never try to drown out other thoughts forcefully, just let them come and go and gently repeat, repeat, repeat the mantra.

Do this twice per day, preferably in the morning before breakfast and in the evening before your last meal. Keep it sacred: please do not share your mantra with anyone.

Hygiene

Your Living Goddess will instruct you on Her pre-ferred practices. An advanced and devoted dasa who wishes to be pleasing to Viola Devi will adhere to the following protocols:

Oil Pulling - done every morning before you brush your teeth:

1. Choose Your Oil: Coconut oil is a popular choice due to its pleasant taste and antimicrobial properties. You can also use sesame or sunflower oil.

2. Swish, Don't Gargle or Swallow: Gently swish 1-2 tablespoons of the oil around your mouth and pull it through your teeth. Avoid gargling or swallowing the oil because it will contain bacteria and toxins drawn from your mouth during the process.

3. Duration: Aim for 15 minutes, but if you're new to oil pulling, start with a shorter duration of 2-5 minutes and gradually increase the time as you become comfortable. You can also try diluting the oil with warm water initially to ease into the sensation.

4. Spit it Out: After swishing, spit the oil into a trash can, not a sink or toilet, as it can clog the pipes as the oil solidifies.

5. Rinse and Brush: Rinse your mouth thoroughly with warm water and then brush your teeth as usual.

Tongue Scraping - Scrape your tongue after brushing your teeth. Follow the directions below. A copper scraper is much preferred as it has antimicrobial qualities.

1. Rinse your scraper. Before you begin, run your tongue scraper under warm water to clean it.

2. Position yourself. Stand in front of a mirror, open your mouth, and stick out your tongue as far as you comfortably can.

3. Place the scraper. Place the rounded end of the scraper at the back of your tongue. If you have a sensitive gag reflex, start closer to the middle and gradually work your way back with practice.

4. Scrape gently. Using light but firm pressure, slowly pull the scraper forward toward the tip of your tongue. Do not scrape backward toward your throat. And don't press too hard as to irritate or injure your tongue.

5. Rinse and repeat. After each pass, rinse the scraper under running water to clear off the bacteria and debris. Repeat the scraping motion 2–5 times, covering the entire surface of your tongue.

6. Wash the scraper after every use. Mild soap and water work best.

Remain Fragrance Free - Choose shampoos, conditioners, lotions, deodorants and other body or skin care products that are fragrance free. Remember to check that it says "fragrance free" on the label and not "unscented." Some manufacturers use a synthetic fragrance deceptively called "unscented" to trick consumers. Fragrances contain endocrine disruptors and can also cause discomfort or distraction. Your Living Goddess may allow specific fragrances with permission or special instruction. For example, Viola Devi enjoys natural vanilla, pistachio, coconut or almond scents. If in doubt, ask permission first.

Body Exfoliation - Using a body brush, you can dry brush your body before bathing. If you are short on time, exfoliate your entire body in the shower or bath with a natural fiber net sponge. Always start at the most outward parts of your limbs and move in toward the heart. Moisturize with a fragrance-free oil, body butter, or lotion (jojoba oil and shea butter are nice) after exfoliating.

Basic Skin Routine - Keep your skin healthy by washing and moisturizing your face in the morning and before bed. Very simple gentle cleansers and face oils are sold in the Gynarchy Shop, but any fragrance-free products you like are fine. If you have facial hair, keep it neatly trimmed and conditioned. Keep your nails clean and neatly trimmed.

Neat Clothing - Do not approach any Living Goddess or Oracle wearing clothing that is ripped or stained or has an odor. Please avoid using scented detergents or fabric softeners and opt for "free and clear" detergents. Your Goddess wants to smell you, not a synthetic fragrance.

Absolute Obedience Routines

Viola Devi's dasas play a game called Absolute Obedience, as described below.

It is a way to exercise your ability to be totally obedient and consistent over a long period of time with a specific protocol. **If you miss a day** or **simply forget to post about it, you have to start all over from the beginning.** You can choose one or two simple protocols to start, or perform one of the 108 Hard or 108 Soft Challenges as outlined below. You may repeat them as often as you like.

Absolute Obedience, protocol # 1

The Pledge - recite your pledge to Viola Devi daily for 108 days straight, no interruptions (if you miss a day, you start over). You may upload an audio file to Her DMs.

After reciting it, go to the #absolute-obedience channel and write:

"I obeyed Viola Devi today, day #xxx."

Absolute Obedience, protocol # 2

This one is called "Daily Sacrifice." Choose something that brings you pleasure but has become a bad habit for you - white sugar, cannabis, alcohol, caffeine, orgasms, a specific food, hobby, anything pleasurable - and give it up in Her honor for 108 days. Many dasas begin with orgasm denial, including either full chastity or edging.

Each day you will go to the #absolute-obedience channel and write:

"I sacrificed for Viola Devi today, day #xxx."

You may share (with Viola Devi or the group) any difficulties you are having in making the sacrifice in your journal and on the Discord channel.

108 CHALLENGE

Want to do more? This is a mental challenge to see if you can obey Viola Devi's protocols for 108 days straight without fail. Can you commit to being consistent?

If you miss a day or forget to log your day, you must start all over.

When you have finished your entire list for the day, *come to the #absolute-obedience channel on the Discord server and write:*

"I did 108 Hard for Viola Devi, day # xxx."

or

"I did 108 Soft for Viola Devi, day # xxx."

108 HARD

1. Record your pledge for Viola Devi every morning or evening and send it to her as a DM.

2. Sit nude and collared in front of your altar and do mantra meditation for 21 minutes at least once (preferably twice) daily.

3. Do an oil pull and use a tongue scraper both morning and night when you brush your teeth.

4. Drink no less than 2 liters (64 ounces) of water per day.

5. Check in to the server to say good morning every day.

6. Sacrifice your orgasms for 108 days straight. You may edge (just be careful! If you orgasm you will need to start over).

7. Log all your calories and macros in your choice of apps and send a screenshot to Viola Devi each night. (Most currently use MyNetDiary)

8. NO alcohol for 108 days straight.

9. Log at least 10,000 steps each day on your pedometer.

10. Do the Daily 50: 50 squats, 50 pushups, 50 lunges, 50-second plank, 50-second wall sit. (Search YouTube for "the Daily 50" to see examples)

11. Journal for no less than 20 minutes.

12. Read at least 10 pages of any book on Viola Devi's recommended reading lists.

108 SOFT

1. Record your pledge for Viola Devi every morning or evening and send it to her via DM.

2. Do an oil pull and use a tongue scraper both morning and night when you brush your teeth.

3. Drink no less than 64 ounces (2 liters) of water per day.

4. Check in to the server to say good morning every day.

5. NO alcohol for 108 days straight.

6. Log at least 6,000 steps each day on your pedometer.

7. Journal for no less than 15 minutes.

Tithing and Gifting

It is the role of the dasas to collectively ensure that all of their Living Goddess's needs are met without exception. You can all work together to make sure that Her expenses for housing, utilities, food, toiletries, healthcare, dental work, car expenses, and all basic necessities are covered. It is also your role to make Her life easier and more enjoyable, so buying gifts from Her wish lists and responding to Her requests and asks is a wonderful way to show devotion when you are able.

You may choose to simply tithe a budgeted amount to Her through the church (30% of which will go toward Her expenses with the rest being used for overhead and savings toward the Hive property). Or you may make an arrangement to pay a specific bill, pay down a debt, or provide a specific service.

If you genuinely don't have the funds to offer, or you want to offer practical service, you may contribute 2-10 hours per week of time to work on various projects that help to bring abundance to the Hive, such as promoting and selling books and merchandise. And you may offer yourself for domestic labor, errands, and odd jobs if you live close to Cathexis House.

If you wish to set up a tithe, do so here:

https://www.devidasa.org/offerings

ADVANCED

Marking

Marking can be an important rite of passage to show your commitment to your Living Goddess. For example, dasas may be asked to accept a ritual cutting of a small V on their body as a gift from Viola Devi, or a special hand-drawn brand. They may also receive a PA piercing as an act of devotion.

beckoning heart tattoo

When accepted into the Hive as a full-time indefinite member, Viola Devi may give a dasa permission to have the beckoning heart tattoo marked on the right inner forearm as a symbol of lifelong devotion.

Rituals and Rites

The following are instructions for a few of our specific Devi Dasas Rituals and Rites of Passage. Some others are kept secret for initiates only.

Daily Pain Ritual

Hormesis is a biological phenomenon where exposure to low doses of a stressor, often harmful at higher doses, can trigger beneficial adaptive responses in organisms. Brief controlled exposures to stressors like intense pain can improve health and resilience. Studies show it improves brain function and even works at a cellular level to improve your resistance to disease and your capacity to heal quickly from injury.

Dasa pain rituals can involve ritual caning, paddling, or whipping by the Living Goddess. There should be a light warm-up of one to three minutes to increase circulation to the buttocks and thighs to prevent serious bruising. After that, the pain Sadhana should last for one or three minutes at high intensity.

If you are unable to participate in such rituals, you can use a sadhu board in place of the impact Sadhana. Some choose to do both of these.

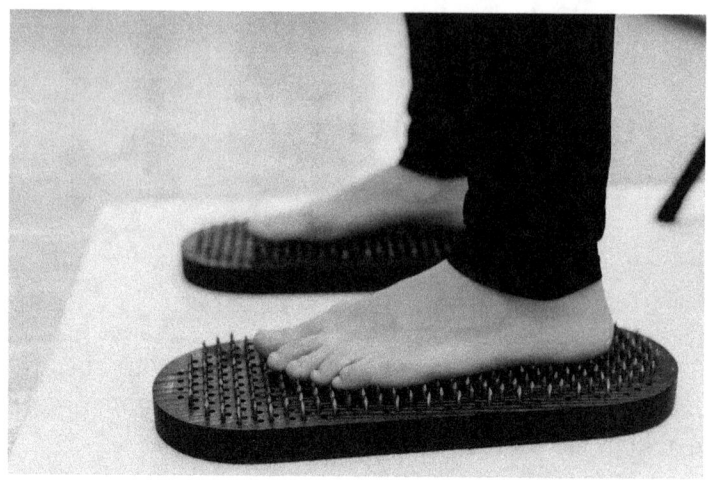

sadhu board

A sadhu board, also known as a "bed of nails" or nail board, is a yoga and meditation tool consisting of a board covered with closely spaced nails. Copper nails are best, but any clean, lead-free nails will work. Beyond physical benefits like improved circulation, sadhu boards are used to quiet the mind, enhance focus, and cultivate mental resilience. The initial discomfort is seen as a way to confront and overcome physical and mental blockages. The practice involves standing on the nails for at least one full minute and then gradually working up to 3, 5, 10, and eventually 20 minutes, often with a focus on breathwork. Some dasas may start with socks and gradually progress to barefoot practice as they become more tolerant of the pain.

The Ending of Covenants

Satsang offered on May 5th, 2024, by Devi Viola Strepsata Voltairine.

> "I make peace, and create evil: I the Lord,
> do all these things." Isaiah 45:7

I have been thinking a lot about how things became twisted. How the institutions of patriarchy marked men as holy and superior and women as sinful and weak. How men came to see us as no more than helpers designed for men's use or wombs to bring forth more men.

The institutions that still today cause some men to perpetuate a sense of entitlement like this are the Abrahamic religions. And the Abrahamic religions are perpetuated by fear of Yahweh and a promise of eternal life if you only obey him. Obedience is the one thing he seeks above all else. His laws need not make sense to you so long as you obey them and fear his wrath for not obeying them. Obey well enough, and you can spend eternity in his presence. You will reach heaven and experience eternal life. This is the covenant he offers.

Yahweh, and what believers call Satan, are both one and the same. They are part of the trap of fear. If you make a covenant with him but do not fear him enough to obey, he will show you something even more frightening to motivate you: Hell, run by a disobedient angel. And this should cause you to want to obey him even more. All the while, his worshipers do not understand that if you do not have a covenant with him, none of it applies to you. You did not buy into the agreement. And you can opt out of the agreement at any moment without consequence. While you are alive here on earth your Mother knows you.

We are not meant to be eternal in the sense that Yahweh offers his worshippers. Devi - The Mother creates us from the absolute silent stillness of non-being and brings us into being. She is the force that animates life. We are each born with the purpose of providing a unique perspective, a unique consciousness, a unique awareness. We each provide the senses through which she gathers knowledge of all life and creation. She is knowledge itself, ever-expanding. We are the eyes, the ears, the tongues, the hands, the bodies that gather knowledge and experience to feed her wisdom. This is our sole purpose for existing.

When we are done, and our bodies have experienced all they can, that which is us, our unique awareness, is blissfully returned to the silent stillness of oblivion from which we came. And new lives are continually created to take our place. All life has a beginning and end and is replaced by new life. From nothing, we are drawn out of the stillness through the sacred doorways of the bodies of women and made into form and consciousness. To nothing, we then return when we have had our fill. Death is just returning to the state we were in before we were born. From the nothing, more life is then created. This is our natural cycle of existence. Just as compost feeds the garden and brings forth food, and then the plants die again and return to the earth as compost. The physical world reflects the nature of Her cycles.

It will surprise many Christians to know that there are those of us who do not want to go to heaven. There are those of us for whom heaven seems an endless torment, no matter how peaceful. Those of us who know that we are not meant to be eternal. That experiencing eternity is a trap. To remain in this unique awareness, this soul self, for eternity, is a form of torture, blocking us from our destination of silent stillness and non-existence after our lives are over. Because all life ends and is replaced with new life. There will be new iterations of us - different and often even better than the previous ones. Memories of us are held in the genes of our children and their children, passed through the mitochondrial DNA of Mothers, who carry our ancestors in their bodies. To be blocked and held back, to experience time eternal in the presence of a god who demands you adhere to his will, is a prison, and he is the authoritarian prison guard.

It may surprise some to know that I do believe that Yahweh exists and will never argue that he doesn't. That which has a real effect on our material existence can be nothing less than real, and Yahweh has had devastating effects on the world. He may be a man-made phenomenon, an egregore created or summoned by collective belief, birthed in the minds of humans and shaped and made active by centuries of worship and fear. Regardless of his origin or source, I do not believe he is good. In fact, all the real and tangible results of his presence among humans have been that of an indisputably malevolent force. In short, he hates the human race, as is evidenced repeatedly in his holy books.

I will have no covenant with him, as it is a trick to keep you trapped with him eternally and never be released into the silence that is our origin. He is not to be trusted. Those who do will pay the price of their soul's freedom. As in the quote from Isaiah, Yahweh is he who creates evil. Not just evil itself, but he creates divisions, causing his worshipers to experience alternating phases of peace and calamity. He makes them see one another as evil and judge one another as inherently sinful for not obeying his every law and command. He pits them against each other. He causes them to engage in conflict with one another, often quite violently, so when they come to an end, he can fulfill that promise of eternity as a slave to his will. His cults are death cults, focused on the end of life and viewing this one precious life as far less important than being with him in eternity. They regard the body, not as a living sensing organ of the divine, but as an adversary to goodness, corrupted and dirty.

Think of how a serial killer, who has caused nothing but suffering in this life, is then welcomed to Yahweh's eternal life if only he makes his covenant with Yahweh in his last days, or even in his last breaths. Yahweh will make permanent, obedient, eternal slaves of anyone he can. He promises to forgive you for the sins about which you carry guilt or shame and welcome you into a peaceful eternity. It is an eternity of experiencing the unending movement of time without any escape, adhering to his will. All the while, those who make such an agreement do not even know that we can all return to the silent, still oblivion when it is all done, with no shame, and no more worldly concerns at all. We can simply dissolve into unity and cease to be. Death is the blissful birthright of all.

Yahweh fights the natural order and is jealous of the Mother's power to create. He claims his followers as his own for all time.

I am here to speak to you with the call of The Mother. You can opt out of this covenant. There are millions around the world who have never even heard of it and suffer nothing from being unaware. You can also break your covenant with him, and nothing bad will happen. In fact, he can no longer expect your obedience to him once you have canceled your agreement. He can no longer punish you for your sins against him. He cannot threaten hell or damnation, for that is only for those who worship him, hold to their covenant with him, and then fail to obey his laws. But after death, if you have made an agreement and kept the covenant with Yahweh, you are trapped eternally. It's horrifying. Imagine experiencing all of time eternally, unable to escape or return to the stillness from which you were created. To exist for all time, never returning home. And to have no will to stray from perfect obedience to him.

If that appeals to you, then that is your destiny. However, if you only remember the natural cycle of the Mother, she will deliver you back to the stillness from which She created you when your time here is done.

Be careful when you make agreements and with whom. Beware of death cults that wish you to focus on life in the hereafter instead of on this precious life here and now. It is always a trap. Remember that you have a choice, and without a covenant, those cults and their god hold no sway over the course of your life. If you put your life in his hands, as they urge you to with great zeal, you have bought your place in eternity with no escape, bound to his will alone. Think carefully and ask if that is what you truly want.

I have created a prayer for those of you who wish your soul, your consciousness, and your lives to be free and to return home to your source when this life is over. Read it and speak it if you want to declare your liberation.

Prayer of Freedom

Please hear me Devi, the Mother of All who brought me forth from absolute silent stillness into this world through the sacred doorway of the body of a woman. I have found my way back and remember You now. I give You my love and gratitude for this life. I speak with reverence as the unique voice and the unique awareness created by Your desire for knowledge.

In your presence, I break the bonds of any and all covenants made by myself, or by others on my behalf that would hold me back from my return to my source. I deny allegiance to any death cults that would draw my attention away from this one precious life that I have been given. I cancel all agreements that would trap me, preventing the natural cycle of my homecoming, and block my reentry into the bliss of the silent stillness from which we all came.

I understand that my purpose is to be a source of experience and knowledge to add to Your ever-expanding wisdom and to bring ease and joy to the other beings with whom I share this brief time. I revere the life-givers and the women who are the sacred doorways of creation, through which not only our physical bodies are brought forth but through whom dreams and new creative visions emerge to bathe us in abundance.

Devi, have mercy and speak to me of Your desire. How shall I best serve You as I move through this life? I ask for Your loving guidance in sweet surrender. Thank You for the gift of this life, and may I be the best and most joyful tool of Your exploration.

With that, know you can always return to your previous covenant if ever you wish to. There is no force or coercion in your Mother's embrace. She is unconditional. There is no punishment for making mistakes. Each of us has free will in all things. No matter how many times you may forget Her and remember Her again, She will love you and provide you a gentle journey home.

The Rite of Isolation

It is important that each dasa has the experience of being alone with nothing but his thoughts so that he may unearth his shadow and the unconscious rumblings that may hold him back from surrender to the Living Goddess. So, the Rite of Isolation should be done at the beginning of his journey as a dasa and may be repeated periodically if needed. It is a total mental reset and detox from the outside world.

This is a simple three-day rite. The dasa stays in one room with a bed, a chair and a private toilet, and with no access to any technology. No phones, no tablets, no TV, no radio, no music, and no books or other reading materials. The only contact he may have with others is someone bringing him specially selected nutritionally complete meal replacement shakes, but they will not speak at all. These shakes will be his only food while in isolation.

The rite consists of 72 hours of very simply resting and sitting with his own thoughts. There is no specific intention or goal. He may do some yoga and meditation whenever he wishes, but he may not speak unless given a specific mantra to repeat by the Living Goddess. He may not write or draw or consume any kind of outside information. He may sleep when he feels like sleeping, eat when he feels like eating, and bathe when he feels like bathing.

At the end of the three days, he will be brought a journal to write or sketch about his experience. He will then join the Living Goddess in the Temple to discuss his reflections before resuming his usual activities.

The Rite of Atonement

The Rite of Atonement is a voluntary rite performed on a dasa when he wishes to acknowledge and try to make amends for the harms inflicted on women by the patriarchy. He must offer himself as a willing sacrifice to absorb some of the pain that women have endured at the hands of men throughout the past 5000 to 10,000 years. His attitude must be sincere, laying down his life as an offering and facing total annihilation by the Living Goddess if necessary. His posture of one of absolute surrender, willing to endure anything done to him as an act of penance for all of his gender.

INSTRUCTIONS

The dasa must fast for 24 hours prior to the Rite, beginning on the evening before the new moon. He should drink plenty of water and may also drink unsweetened caffeine-free tea if he chooses. He must prepare a small gift, some small valuable object that is important to him and represents a true sacrifice on his part.

The following evening, he presents himself naked to the Living Goddess in the Temple. He lays with his body face down and as flat to the ground as possible, his right arm extended toward her.

Living Goddess: *You may kneel and speak.*

Dasa (kneeling, eyes cast downward): *Divine Goddess, I beg to offer myself in a Rite of Atonement for the pain and subjugation of all women.*

Living Goddess: *Do you understand what that means? You must endure suffering and lay down your life to me with open eyes and an open heart.*

Dasa: *Yes, Goddess, I understand and consent, with open eyes and open heart. I mourn for the suffering caused by those of my gender and am ready to sacrifice myself.*

Living Goddess: *Do you have an offering?*

Dasa: *My offering.*

The dasa presents the offering he brought, eyes still cast downward and explains why it represents a significant sacrifice for him.

Living Goddess: *Rise and be anointed.*

The dasa rises to his feet, eyes still cast to the ground as the Goddess anoints him. Here She may use an oil or specially prepared water of Her choice.

She touches it to his third eye point and says:

Blessed be your mind that you may know Devi.

She touches it to his lips and throat and says:

Blessed be your voice that you may speak Her truth.

She touches it to his heart and says:

Blessed be your heart that it may open with over-flowing love for your Goddess.

She touches it to his genitals and says:

Blessed be your loins that you may feel pleasure in worshipping your Goddess.

She touches it to his knees:

Blessed be your knees that kneel at the altar.

She touches it to his feet and says:

Blessed be the feet that walk upon the path that your Goddess has shown you.

She holds his hands in Hers, bringing them together at his heart for a moment, and recites the five ways: **surrender, submit, sacrifice, serve, survive**

He responds:

To Her, for Her, through Her.

Living Goddess: *Do you wish to choose the instruments of atonement?*

Here she will have a number of pain inflicting instruments laid out for him to gaze on. He may choose the ones he consents to have used on him, or he may say the following.

Dasa: *The choice is not mine to make.*

From this point, the Living Goddess will instruct the dasa to take whatever positions She wishes. If other women are present, they may join in the rite. He will be whipped, beaten, cut, bitten, pierced, scratched, trampled, degraded, and otherwise subjugated by the women present in any way they see fit and until they have had their fill. If the mood strikes, they may speak or scream with rage about the harms that women have endured and demand his apology over and over.

The Living Goddess will pay close attention to make sure no permanent damage is done to him, but the female participants are encouraged to let out all of their pent-up suffering, past pain, and frustrations so that the dasa may absorb as much as possible and relieve them.

When the frenzy comes to an end, the Living Goddess will be seated and guide the dasa into Her loving arms. She will hold him and speak softly to him, kissing his forehead. She will envelop him with love. There may be tears from the dasa and the participants.

The rite is closed with Her words of appreciation.

Living Goddess: *Your trial is done. Your sacrifice is acknowledged and accepted with gratitude. I am pleased with your selflessness and devotion. I give you sustenance. You have earned your place in my heart and at my feet.*

Dasa: *Thank you, Divine Goddess.*

She feeds the dasa some water and specially prepared oat cakes to break his fast. If he has wounds, they are cleaned and dressed. When She is satisfied that he is physically and emotionally recovered, She releases him from the Temple.

Rebirth Ritual

The purpose of the rebirth ritual is for a dasa to have a fresh start in his new life as a devoted servant of the Living Goddess. It is not unlike a baptism or similar initiations in other religions. The rebirth ritual should be performed once, either on the dasa's actual birthday or on a new moon. It may last anywhere from 30 minutes to two hours.

PREPARATION

The ritual requirements: A blindfold that seals out all light, soft towels and blankets, a warm bath prepared with coconut milk and any fragrant herbs the Living Goddess choses, and a bottle or glass of fresh room temperature drinking water in case the dasa gets dry mouth. The Living Goddess may select music for the occasion or do the ritual in silence.

If the dasa is to take a new name, the Living Goddess should have selected it well in advance.

The dasa should fast or eat only one light meal in the 24 hours preceding the ritual. He should be sure to remain well-hydrated.

THE RITUAL

The dasa presents himself to the Living Goddess, naked, in the turtle position, holding an offering of a flower.

The Living Goddess sets the intention.

Living Goddess: *Today is the day of your rebirth into a new identity as my beloved dasa. By the blessings of Devi, you have been given a clean slate to begin your new life in service and devotion. Today, I invoke the Mother of All and give you purpose.*

Dasa: *Thank you, Divine Goddess. I am yours.*

Living Goddess: *Rise and be anointed*

The dasa rises to his feet, eyes still cast to the ground as the Goddess anoints him. Here She may use an oil or specially prepared water of Her choice.

She touches it to his third eye point and says:

Blessed be your mind that you may know Devi.

She touches it to his lips and throat and says:

Blessed be your voice that you may speak Her truth.

She touches it to his heart and says:

Blessed be your heart that it may open with over-flowing love for your Goddess.

She touches it to his genitals and says:

Blessed be your loins that you may feel pleasure in worshipping your Goddess.

She touches it to his knees:

Blessed be your knees that kneel at the altar.

She touches it to his feet and says:

Blessed be the feet that walk upon the path that your Goddess has shown you.

She holds his hands in Hers, bringing them together at his heart for a moment, and recites the five ways:

surrender, submit, sacrifice, serve, survive

He responds:

To Her, for Her, through Her.

The Living Goddess guides the dasa into the warm coconut milk bath and places the flower in the water with him. She blindfolds him and helps him settle in and relax. He must be in a comfortable position, with his head well above water, and body fully or mostly submerged.

Once comfortable, the Goddess guides him in the proper breathing technique.

He begins breathing slightly more deeply and more quickly than his normal breath. He should preferably breathe through his mouth for the entire ritual.

He should concentrate on breathing into his heart, expanding his chest without tensing his shoulders or neck.

The breathing should be circular with no pause between breaths. Just a continuous ocean tide-like pattern in and out.

At the prompting of the Goddess, he will speed up the breath, focusing primarily on the inhale, and simply letting go with the exhale, again with the continuous circular pattern and no pauses between.

Here the process becomes more individualized and directed by the Living Goddess. He will continue with this quick circular chest breathing for anywhere from 15 minutes to 90 minutes. The Living Goddess will feel into his journey, as he may start to experience strange sensations, huge emotional waves, or even hallucinations. He may laugh or cry or moan. She will use touch and Her voice to continue to direct the experience.

When She feels the process is complete, She will guide him back into normal breathing until he is still and relaxed. At this point, She will remove the blindfold and guide him to submerge his head under water completely for at least the count of ten. Then She will pull him back up, holding his head in both hands. She will look directly into his eyes.

Living Goddess: *In the love of Devi, you are reborn, and you are mine. (If he has a new name) You will now be known as [new name].*

Dasa: *I am [new name], and I am yours.*

The Living Goddess will guide Her dasa from the tub, dry him and swaddle him in towels and warm blankets. She will close the ritual by holding him and discussing his experience. She may ask him to journal or sketch about the experience before returning to his usual activities. She may also plan a dinner or some other celebration and reintroduce him to the community.

OTHER RITES AND RITUALS

There are many other rites and rituals performed by the dasa within the Devi Dasa Sacred Gynarchy, and given to the dasa as he progresses on his journey.

These include:

The Rite of Ophion - wherein the dasa and Living Goddess stage a reenactment of the first known creation story of Eurynome and Ophion, and the dasa is transformed into a serpent, slithering on his belly in ecstatic reverence.

The Blue Lotus Ritual - wherein the dasa is taught how to interact with the living Goddess in dreams.

The Nightly Bonding Ritual - wherein the dasa is given a recorded hypnotic message from the Living Goddess to listen to every night before going to sleep to intensify their bond even over long distances.

"PRACTICUM" JOURNAL TOPICS

1. What compels you to become a dasa? What emotions and sensations do you feel around committing to this role?

2. What might get in the way of devotion and how can you overcome those obstacles?

3. Which benefits of devotion do you crave or look forward to?

4. Describe your personal relationship to masculinity, and how does being a dasa change that relationship?

5. Explain why the physical is spiritual.

6. List any expectations or protocols that seem challenging for you and why.

7. Describe any honest thoughts, emotional responses, or sensations that you have when reading about the rituals and rites.

8. Describe your relationship with and thoughts about religion in general and why you choose Devi Dasa Sacred Gynarchy as your spiritual path.

SACRED TEXTS

The following are the foundational texts of the Devi Dasa Sacred Gynarchy. Take your time absorbing them and committing the philosophy and concepts contained within to memory.

The Devi Doctrine

The new and ancient religion of Gynarchy.

Originally published in October 2023 in The Pillars of Gynarchy.

On the appropriation of language.

The Devi Doctrine incorporates a lot of words in the Sanskrit language to talk about various ideas and practices. There may be some who voice an objection to this and consider it cultural appropriation. However, almost every religion today is universal, and its adherents use the ancient languages of their religions regardless of where they live. New Muslims in America use the word Allah for their god and speak the Shahada in Arabic in order to convert. Studied Taoists in the West still use Chinese terms like "wu wei" because the English translations seem insufficient or too wordy. Jewish converts use phrases in Hebrew like Shabbat and Shalom, and Western Buddhists use words like Maya and Dharma, which are also Sanskrit terms. It might also be interesting to note that most Indians and Hindus no longer speak Sanskrit, and scholars work hard to preserve it as well as the essential ancient texts written in it. So, though it comes from Indian culture, more Indians speak English than Sanskrit.

Many concepts herein originate within traditions first recorded in the Sanskrit language. They are important and relevant concepts. I could use not-quite-equivalent English terms or make up new words for these very old ideas, but it seems more respectful to maintain them in their original form and allow their meanings to resonate through their sounds. Because everything is sound.

Para Vidya

Higher Knowledge

1 Devi

All known creation is vibration. Nada Brahma - all is sound. Devi is the vibration of creation from which all matter, energy, thought, feeling, sensation, and movement is formed. She is The Mother of All, the life force that shapes us, animates us, and gives us conscious awareness.

Throughout time, all human cultures have known of The Mother, though some have forgotten. That Mother is the symbolic expression of Devi. She has many forms and many names and is embodied in many places at once, in stone and bronze, in art, in nature, and in flesh. Each aspect of her, new and old, is a unique expression to be worshiped as a deity.

In the state of the silent, still, undefined, and absolute potential She is Siva - literally "that which is not." We can immerse ourselves in this infinite and boundless state through meditation, trance, or death. It is our built-in reset program which rescues our minds and nervous systems from chaos and overstimulation. The more practiced we become, the more we can carry the boundlessness, peace, and silence with us into everyday life.

2 Desire

Desire To Be is the cause and motivation of all existence. It is that which caused the differentiation between "that which is" and "that which is not."

Desire to Know - to answer the question "What am I?"- created a third state, making all the infinite iterations of creation possible. It allowed for the threefold division of knower, knowing, and known to materialize, and made variations of thought, form, and movement erupt into being. Every facet and every detail is its own piece of information meant to answer Devi's question, "What am I?" She answers Herself: "I am this, and I am this, and I am this, and I am this..."

The Desire to Know in humans activates within us to show us the nature of existence. All self-conscious beings possess the Desire to Know. The Desire to Know is symbolized in the form of the serpent, who sleeps coiled within and is awakened.

3 Lila (Play)

All that lives and exists in the universe is the infinite creative play of Devi, meant to be marveled at and enjoyed to the fullest. Don't be fooled. Even that which appears serious or grim is just part of Her game. And therefore, there is never need for fear and anxiety.

The opposite of fear is Love. Love is taking the concerns of the other as your own. Love of Devi is identifying with and surrendering to Devi so as to know Her. That Love negates and neutralizes fear.

Our ultimate purpose as humans is to be a channel for Devi's Desires. We are mechanisms by which She creates and expands. If we can sit quietly and listen, allowing logic and reason to fall away, the subtle vibrations of all of Her emerging Desires will move through us effortlessly and become clear.

Her Desires come through us in actions and expressions of self which are authentic, and through our unique and autonomous perspectives. Resisting or blocking the flow of Her Desire creates inevitable challenges and dams up creativity.

Devi's essential qualities are: creative, abundant, cyclical, playful, active, attractive, and sensual. All objects, actions, or energies that may stifle or pervert these qualities are simply obstacles which prevent us from being fully attuned to Devi. Look to the Dark Feminine to find and remove the obstacles.

4 The Trellis and the Flowering Vine

Devi, the Divine Feminine, has no equal or opposite.

She created the divine masculine for a purpose.

First, he is the trellis to Her flowering vine. Without the trellis, the vine will still grow, but with it, the vine takes new shapes and directions and thrives, reaching ever toward the light. Without the trellis, the vine is more vulnerable to that which can harm it, and its fruits might lay on the ground and decay.

The trellis alone without the vine stands with no purpose, upright and casting a long shadow, but easier to blow over without the weight of the vine wrapped around it. It is a scaffolding without a use. Structural and stoic, without lush beauty and growth.

Because he gives Her snaking tendrils the lines and angles on which to hold, he plays a second role. He is her witness and scribe, the translator of metaphor into math, of symbol into words. He finds underlying logic in Her patterns and rhythm in Her pulses and waves.

He remembers. He creates shorthand. He stores memory in bits, encoded as ones and zeros so She can easily call up lost passwords and combinations. She is raw data, and he is the formula that describes and organizes it.

5 Woman and Man

Likewise, Devi created Woman to populate the Earth and be an agent of Her Desire. She engendered the Desire to Know coiled within Her, and Consciousness of Self and Awareness of Others in order that she might play, engage, enjoy, and ponder all of creation.

Woman, too, is a creator. She is Devi of the flesh. When she forgets this, or when her power is bound too tightly or oppressed, She suffers.

Thereafter Devi created man from the body of Woman and in the image of Woman, as an expression of the divine masculine, to lend variety and stability to Woman. The genes he contributes to the creation of other humans act as a protection against disease.

Man was created to support and love Her, and to be the enchanted witness to creation and describe, count, and catalog all that he sees.

He is the tooth of the serpent - he who is shaped by the Desire to Know, but who, without Love of Devi, becomes a lost fragment, not privy to the bigger picture.

6 The Devi and the dasa

The Living Goddess is the embodiment of the Divine Feminine. The center of Her spiritual Hive. She fully acknowledges that She is Devi Herself in differentiated and consecrated form, as a human Woman. She is both fully human and fully divine.

She has made herself a clear and open conduit for Devi's Desire, while at the same time maintaining a perspective unique to her place in time and context.

Her many human faults make Her a deity that one can see, hear, touch, and relate to. Without them, She would be made of stone. But at times She will seem distant and will need long periods of quiet meditation to remain grounded in everyday reality while being ever attuned to Desire.

The dasa is the ultimate expression of the divine masculine. He is supportive in every way, facilitating ease and flow, adding stability, order, and security to the life of his Living Goddess.

He is a witness to Her, fully and deeply aware of Her divinity, paying careful attention and recording both Her Desires and Her acts of creation. More than an average devotee, he has made Her his life's focus.

In turn, She has opened his heart wide, tamed his ego, and led him to better understand the nature of his existence and his reason for being. He is fully able to take on Her concerns as if they were his own, and he will take on any task or any role in order to bring Her pleasure and joy.

He is sometimes the messenger between the Living Goddess and others, a protective layer to keep Her annoyances and distractions to a minimum.

7 Laboratory Earth

The universe which sprang from Devi has in it a laboratory, a sandbox within which contrasts and compliments are mixed and matched in endless experimental glee. The laboratory is Earth, and there is nothing in the universe like it, with the conditions made just right for the ripening of Desire in three dimensions.

The lab is sealed off to maintain the integrity of the experiment, and the dimensions beyond its doors can scarcely be imagined by the humans within. Though self-aware they are sealed in, with only the device of the mind to probe limits beyond their senses.

That is until the Desire to Know uncoils, fully awake within them, to give them a different kind of sight.

The Purpose

Here

The point and purpose of living is to experience and enjoy the awe-inspiring variety and complexity of Devi's ongoing and endless creation.

In doing so, you are able to love Devi, be a conduit and tool of Her Desires, and realize unity with Her in a very real way. This eliminates fear and anxiety.

When in love with Devi, the vibration that makes up your being, consciousness and body are tuned to be in complete harmony with everything around you. You experience a feeling of connection to all. Conflicts fall away, and your intelligence, awareness, and empathy increase. Creativity, abundance, and ease envelop you.

This is not a difficult path if you are able to simply remember. Remember the Mother.

Devi consciousness uncoils the serpent within, and the Desire to Know fully awakens. You gain knowledge of what moves beyond the laboratory Earth. You gain an understanding of the bigger picture, which cannot be described in the language of words.

Hereafter

The Devi Doctrine does not teach a concept of an afterlife, nor heaven or hell. In death, like a drop of water in a vast ocean, "that which is you" returns to merge into Siva - "that which is not." Reincarnation exists only in the fact that every bit of energy that is created gets cycled and recycled into something new. The energy that animates you and gives you conscious awareness is no different.

You are but a mechanism, or a program, designed to gain a unique perspective on the answer to Devi's question "What am I?"

The goal in this life becomes orchestrating a connected existence of exuberance and fearless exploration while learning to understand what you are, as well as what lies beyond the senses. There are mysteries unspoken.

Energetic and emotional echoes and reverberations of your unique presence remain on Earth forever, as well as any acts of creation you contributed to the planet, be they knowledge, art, or human offspring. What echoes and traces will you leave behind?

Bhakti

Actions/Behaviors of the Devotee

The Devi Doctrine is primarily a path of devotion or "Bhakti." But action, knowledge, and direct experience play significant roles. The Bhakti path removes arrogance, jealousy, anger, hatred, and egoism and replaces them with divine ecstasy, bliss, and wisdom.

The Devi devotee seeks to open the heart and release fear and open the eyes and see what is real. Being given a point of focus, someone to whom they can surrender - a Living Goddess in which to pour their love and service - is a true gift to a devotee. It clears the path, smooths the road, and puts them on a fast track to a fulfilled existence.

When you find your Living Goddess, you know. You are filled with something akin to obsession. It is called Cathexis. Cathexis is a prerequisite to falling in love. Cathexis is the heart-opening process and love is the result. Cathexis is the feeling that makes you keep the Living Goddess foremost in your thoughts because you cannot help otherwise. It focuses life energy in a singular direction, like the inner compass pointing true North. It sets the stage for devotion.

You may dream of Her. You may hear Her voice in your head when you are alone. Your thoughts always return to Her. These are signs that She is your Living Goddess and you should approach and offer your devotion and service.

A devotee who has committed fully may earn the honor of being called "dasa" by their Living Goddess. It means servant of the deity, or one who has surrendered to the deity. It has been translated as "slave" though it has nothing to do with non-consensual chattel slavery.

As the devotee steps onto the path, however, they may face challenges within them which create a detour or pause their journey. These are quite normal and can be overcome.

The 4 Internal Challenges

The Challenge of Impatience

When one finds their Goddess, it can lead to a feeling of frenzy. You want to do everything. You want to know everything about Her. And you need it all to happen right now. Your only want is to be in Her presence or in constant contact at all times and absorb all you can. Enjoy the feeling, but do not allow yourself to become agitated and impatient when things don't move as quickly or as intensely as you would like. Your Goddess may first deliberately test your patience before offering up any other lessons. Allow the frenzy to settle into a steady, easy hum that propels you through your day.

The Challenge of Entitlement

If stuck in a transactional mindset, one might feel that when one is doing so many things to please and serve the Goddess, one must be entitled to some small thing in return. That something could be Her time and attention, words of praise, a smile, acknowledgment, favored treatment, or quick responses to one's email. It is this sense of entitlement that creates uncomfortable feelings of resentment, not the Goddess Herself. Her only obligation is to allow you to view Her as an object of veneration and graciously accept the love you pour into Her, that your heart may open and your ego lay down in obedience when in Her presence.

The Challenge of Centering

To adjust to the Bhakti path you must begin to pay close attention to where you center your perspective. You may be surprised at how often you view yourself as the main character in the whole universe's story. How often can you catch yourself recognizing that you've centered your wants, your needs, your values, your expectations, and your point of view? The Goddess provides you the opportunity to grow your empathy ten thousandfold. And you do this by simply re-centering your perspective with Her as the central character. It takes careful study but try to begin to see everything from the perspective of Her values, wants, needs, vision, and point of view. You will find your mind expanded.

The Challenge of Ennui

One must face the fact that often being a devotee can be tedious. You may be asked to engage in repetitive routines and rituals. You may have to do tasks and drudgework that is not particularly stimulating. Don't let boredom set you off course. If you forget that each and every action is an act of love and devotion, you may begin to moan, whine and complain. In doing so, you tell your Goddess that what she wants from you is unimportant and that Her wishes are putting you out when you could be doing so many more fun and interesting things. Instead, focus on doing everything well and with conscious intention, even waiting for your next instructions.

The Remedies

There are certain disciplines and practices that are key to gaining the sense of closeness and unity that you desire with your Goddess. They are remedies to your inevitable internal challenges that remind you of your place and your purpose.

Nandi

The concept of Nandi is named after the bull Vahana (mount, or vehicle) belonging to Shiva, the Adi Yogi (that means original yogi, in contrast to Siva, which is the broader concept of "that which is not."). He is meant to show devotees the proper attitude.

Shiva was known to go into deep meditation for very long periods of time - possibly thousands of years. Nandi, his bull, would sit waiting for him, a contented look on his face, resting, with one hoof raised and ready to stand at any moment. His waiting was not passive. He was not sleeping. It was an active, aware, and alert kind of waiting. If Shiva changed his facial expression, Nandi would notice. He was ready to spring into action and be of service whenever needed. The contented look on his face showed that he was willing to wait forever without complaint. To overcome impatience and ennui, practice being like the bull Nandi. Challenge yourself to ever-extended times of sitting in alert patience or mantra meditation without falling asleep.

Seva

Seva means selfless service. This is not service done to make yourself feel righteous for having been such a good and kind person. It is done without any motives other than the act of service itself. It is utterly empty of transactional thought or expectations. It's not done for personal gain or to gain favor or gratitude from others. It is plainly motivated by the wish to serve. It helps to get ego out of your way and to increase empathy and attunement to the needs of others. To practice selfless service, you only ask what needs to be done, and do it. In doing so, you may feel a strange sense of immeasurable joy, which may become addictive. But don't go in with that feeling as your end goal. Approach it as a service for the sake of service alone. It is also important that you not use it to judge and compete with others, comparing notes on who serves more. This is a great remedy to decenter yourself and remove feelings of entitlement. It also keeps you from getting bored and occupies your time so you can avoid impatience.

Puja

Puja is a daily ritual of devotion. The devotee keeps an altar and sits before it in communion with his Goddess (or Goddesses). Usually, there will be an image of Her at the center, or a symbol representing Her. First, he will cleanse his body. He will bow deeply in reverence to her image and strike or ring a bell or gong. Then he will offer the elements (incense as air, lamp or candle as fire, water, and salt or something of substance grown in earth, as well as an oil to represent ether) and other gifts such as flowers, coins, perfume, fruits, sweets, etc. The gifts should be significant to his individual Goddess. This is followed by Her favorite mantras, reciting Her name 108 times, and/or a pledge to the Goddess which She has written for this purpose. Only if instructed by Her, he may engage in self-flagellation to remind him to remain disciplined, or masturbation (without orgasm) to raise erotic energy as an offering to Her. And, if there is time, this is followed by a period of meditation and/or contemplation on the Goddess. He will end the puja with another deep bow or by laying his body face down on the floor to position himself as low as possible before Her image, and a final ringing of the bell. Puja is a beautiful reminder of your place and purpose and will ease the frenzied or agitated mind.

Darshan

Darshan is looking upon or making visual contact with the deity or holy person. In person, Darshan can often involve a lesson given by the Goddess, or a discussion where She answers questions. The devotee will sit at Her feet and gaze upon her intently. If he is lucky, She will make eye contact, which is a powerful form of blessing, personally acknowledging the love and service of the devotee. Some Goddesses will allow the devotee or devotees to bow and kiss, anoint, or worship Her feet. It is the direct interaction between devotee and Deity. But Darshan need not be in person. One may receive Darshan by simply gazing upon an image - a photo or drawing - of his Goddess, looking deeply into Her eyes. It is often enough to bring about incredible feelings of love and an altered state of consciousness for the devotee. And doing so while also hearing a recording of Her voice can feel no different than if She were there in person. In some more powerful instances of Darshan, the devotee may feel compelled to cry, laugh, dance, moan, or even flail on the floor in ecstasy. He may feel he has been shot into outer space. This is a powerful remedy to decenter the self, and will cure any sense of mental agitation, fear, or ennui.

The Five Steps

Symbolized as the five circling petals of the hibiscus flower, there are five steps the devotee takes upon entering the service of a Living Goddess. They are taken in order.

Surrender

The first step is necessary before any of the others. This is the realization that you truly want your life to be led by the Living Goddess. You sincerely have no wish to be in control. In trust, with open eyes and an open heart, you let go of fear and surrender to Her Desire.

Submit

Yield to Her authority and put up no resistance. You say yes. You learn to know Her. Your ego lies down quietly at Her feet, and you obey Her.

Sacrifice

Sacrifice things that once felt important but no longer have meaning or do not serve you on your path. Superficial attachments dissolve. For Her, you can release what needs to be released. You realize the insignificance of minor matters that once loomed large.

Serve

Be of practical use in making Her life better, easier, and more pleasurable. Find pleasure in your ability to be useful and competent and take on every task as an act of love. Serve without expectation.

Survive

This is both the survival of human life on Earth renewed by our devotion to the Feminine, and the survival of your spiritual commitment to Devi. You persist and endure, your steps steady and assured.

Behaviors of the Living Goddess

Embodying Love

A Living Goddess must be able to allow people to love Her. This may be harder than it sounds. It is an active process of attracting and drawing out love from another, cleaving their heart wide open. It is allowing Her power as the embodiment of love itself to flow freely through Her and reach out and pull others in seemingly effortlessly, like a vortex. It means being unperturbed and unafraid when someone falls to Her feet and proclaims that he is Hers. She must fall in love freely and often whenever She sees someone's heart. She is capable of experiencing all flavors of love. But She must also be able to sit firm in Her own power of Desire, not allowing the desires of others to sway Her away from Her own. Her Desire is the ultimate guide. It is the Desire of Devi moving through Her. She has the unique privilege and responsibility of being the catalyst for Her devotees' spiritual evolution, and the focus of their efforts.

Devi's Desire

A Living Goddess is an agent of Devi's Desire. Devi's Desire is not an immutable proclamation from on high; not the "will of the gods" unfathomable and imposing. For the Living Goddess, to know Devi's Desire is to simply sit with the question "What do I want?" And it may begin very small. "I want a drink of water." But as the Living Goddess becomes more practiced at asking, She will find the larger answers which resonate like the strike of a gong through her entire being. It is not an analytical process of reasoning and guessing what She wants. She allows the answers to come to Her and checks them for authenticity. "Is this what I want?" What She wants will move Her. The answers for every Living Goddess will be different because She is a unique expression of Devi. But if answers align among Goddesses, a broader Desire is being expressed.

Consecration

Consecration of the Living Goddess can happen in many ways. It may happen through Her own long and steady Sadhana (spiritual practice: meditation, trance, puja, etc.) that She comes to the moment when She realizes Her readiness. It may happen without warning, like a bolt out of the blue, that She enters a trance, sees the design of existence laid out before Her, and instantly knows Her role in it. This is spontaneous Shaktipat (a transference of spiritual experience or awareness) from Devi Herself. She may also be consecrated by another Living Goddess, receiving Shaktipat from Her, and may even be mentored in creating Her Temple and Hive. Consecration is the alchemical process of becoming holy and sacred, of becoming fully conscious of the self as Divine, of the self as Devi. It is common for devotees to refer to a consecrated Woman simply as Devi or Devi either followed by or following her first name (Viola Devi or Devi Viola are both appropriate, for example).

Every Woman has the innate potential to be realized as a Living Goddess; a few are born wielding this power from day one. Not every woman will want to be consecrated as a Living Goddess, as she has a different path to take and different concerns, and she does not wish to take on the responsibility of becoming the central focus of the devotion of many. However, obstacles to a Woman's wish to be consecrated might be issues of ego. Either she has become mired in the perverse feminine and wants to be worshiped out of the need to feel important and to use her power over others to assuage her feelings of insecurity, or her insecurity and lack of self-knowledge make her feel unworthy. The motivation to become a Living Goddess will emerge from a sincere wish to serve and lead others and from a profound understanding of Devi's Desire.

The Holy Humanness of the Goddess

It is important for the Living Goddess to maintain Her humanity. She should show Her devotees that she feels the full spectrum of human emotion and is capable of real empathy. She should eat, breathe, shit, and orgasm as a Woman, and enjoy all aspects of Her human existence. She is still a one-of-a-kind participant in the infinite multiplicity and diversity of the planet. Her intuition will be heightened and Her perspective on all of existence broadened, but Her body of flesh and blood is still crucial in Her role. She may be more inclined to live a healthy lifestyle, but She can suffer illness and injury just as Her devotees suffer.

There are no hard and fast protocols on how a Living Goddess must speak or behave. Each is marvelously unique. Her purpose is to attract specific devotees who can attune to Her Desires and who wish to have a living human Woman onto which to focus their feelings of love, devotion, and service. Divine love becomes a fully embodied experience of Divinity, not an abstract one. Humans can begin their spiritual evolution through the worship of a statue of stone or bronze; however, Women are the natural embodiment of love for human beings, beginning with our first feelings for our mothers when we are infants. It is a comforting path for most.

There will be times a Living Goddess begins to lose Her human inclinations. When this happens, She will dive deep into extended meditation, lasting days or weeks. During these times, She is exploring and expanding, gaining new wisdom, tracing new energetic channels between Her and devotees or other Goddesses, or recharging Herself to emerge again with greater energy. Or She may be preparing to leave. A Goddess of very old age or experiencing terminal illness will eventually stop communicating with devotees directly. She will spend more and more time in meditation, resting on the subtle edge of "that which is not." It is best not to disturb Her during these times, but to carry on with your devotions.

Sacred Practices and Rites

Along with the essential concepts of Nandi, Seva, Puja, and Darshan, there are many other rites and practices that may be a part of life in a Gynarchic Hive. Each Living Goddess should keep Her own private Book of Rites with more detailed instructions for carrying out sacraments, ceremonies, and rituals. These are best not made public in order to protect the sanctity of each Hive's religious system. But within the congenial Gynarchy network, the Goddess may reach out to gain knowledge from other Living Goddesses. Her own knowledge and Her Desires will shape the spiritual culture of Her hive. There will be practices that are specific to each Hive, but most will participate in at least some version of the following:

Meditation

Mantra meditation is effective at bringing the practitioner closer and closer to the most subtle vibration of existence, thereby allowing them to reset their nervous system and bring the peace of Siva out into their everyday life. Mantras should only be given to the meditator by their Goddess and will be a bija or "seed" mantra (or a string of seed mantras). These are words in Sanskrit chosen for the specific power of the vibration of their sounds. It is best to keep the mantra secret between the meditator and their Goddess and not share it with others. During the initial meditation, the mantra is first repeated out loud. It is repeated in progressively quieter tones until it is barely audible. It is then repeated only within the mind, silently. After the first meditation, it never needs to be spoken out loud again except at the request of a Goddess.

Sitting comfortably with the eyes closed, and breathing normally, the meditator repeats the mantra mentally for 21 minutes, allowing all thoughts to come and go without trying to direct them or force them away. If the devotee gets lost in thought, they should gently return to the repetition of the mantra. It should feel effortless. At the end of 21 minutes, the meditator stops the repetition, sits with eyes closed for one to two minutes, and then gently comes back to their normal waking state. The point of the meditation is to occupy the space between waking and sleep for long periods, which causes brainwave coherence and a total refresh of the entire nervous system. If possible, this should be done twice daily, in the morning and late afternoon or evening.

Cyclical Rites

Full and New Moon Rituals

The Divine Feminine is cyclical. And our calendars used to be kept by looking at the moon. The full moon is a time when energies are at their peak and about to subside, and it is a good time for letting go of what no longer serves you. The new moon is the best time to state intentions and begin new endeavors, using the pull of the waxing moon to add momentum. The new moon is also an excellent time to engage in dream rituals as the lack of reflected sunlight means sleep is deeper and less disturbed.

Solstice and Equinox Celebrations

The Solstices are when we experience the longest and shortest days of the year, and the equinoxes are the midpoint in between. Since the beginning of agrarian society, we have marked these times as times for planting and harvesting, feasting and rest. The Winter Solstice celebrates the return of the sun, as days begin growing longer, so festivals of light are common around the world. At the Spring Equinox, the ground begins to thaw, seeds begin to sprout, and we celebrate rebirth and renewal, a time full of color. The Summer Solstice celebrates the peak of fertility, with sexual and transformative rites. And the Autumnal Equinox is time for a great harvest feast and to celebrate the abundance of diverse expressions of Devi.

Celebration of the Birth of the Living Goddess

The birthday of your personal Living Goddess is a time for celebration and gratitude. You serve Her well all year, but at this time it is time to stop everything and just recognize the important role She plays in your life. Devotees should place the Goddess upon a throne, surrounded by opulence and beauty, and make offerings of things She loves. Write poetry and songs in Her honor and enjoy a feast of her favorite foods. Look to this day as your Hive's New Year.

Yoni Puja

Yoni puja is the worship of the yoni - the female sexual anatomy, as the symbol of the cosmic source of all. The yoni of a Woman at the peak fertile time of her cycle is preferred, although sculptures and yoni-shaped stones may be used in her place. Men occupying their "animal nature" and not ready to show respect and reverence should not be included. There are similarities to daily puja, with elemental offerings and gifts and mantras chanted. Liquids are poured over the yoni and collected in a vessel, and the resulting mixture is sipped by all participants. Participants may make wishes upon the yoni or ask for blessings, and then there is a period of contemplation of the yoni before the puja is done.

Menses

Menses are the time of rest for all Women. A Woman may mark her "red tent days" (the time of heaviest bleeding, usually at the start of her cycle) as times when she is not to be expected to take on any responsibilities. She should not even be expected to cook food for herself. This is a dedicated time for relaxation and extra pampering. She may get massages and enjoy free bleeding either in her own tub, outside in the garden (menstrual blood is great for fertilizing plants), or in a section of a warm bath house dedicated to this purpose. She may lay naked and be washed with hot flowing waters as she unlocks her pelvic muscles and releases all tension.

Rites of Passage

Isolation and Embrace

Every Hive should have a quiet room equipped with a shower, toilet, comfortable mattress, and a chair, with plain undecorated white walls. Every new initiate to the Hive must spend between 3 and 9 days alone, with no screens, no books, no entertainment, and no human interaction beyond the silent delivery of plain but healthy meals like quinoa, oats, soups, and smoothies.

We all must understand what kind of madness we suffer. This isolation period allows one to get in touch with one's own mind, untangle one's anxieties and neurosis, and understand our levels of patience and coping skills. It's also a detox from the noise of the world, a way to clear one's head.

Slowly books, music, and writing implements will be reintroduced to the initiate. Plant medicines may be administered, such as Bobinsana to help remove melancholy from the brain. They will then be brought out by the Queen and greeted by a small group of 3-5 members who have been through the same or similar process. The initiate will have an opportunity to process all the thoughts and feelings that moved through them during isolation and talk about ways to soothe their demons. They may go on walks and engage in physical exercise, and they will be given warm embraces to welcome them into the fold. After spending some time with the small group, they will be introduced to the larger community with a celebratory meal and given their own room or living space. The initiate may be given a day to acclimate before taking over any jobs or responsibilities they've been given, or, if they wish, they may be trained right away and jump right into the rhythm of the Hive.

Naming Ceremony

Upon being accepted into a Hive, Women are supported in choosing their own name, and their surname can be changed to the first name of a Woman in their family or a woman they admire. They may also choose to change their entire name or, conversely, affirm their love for their given name. Men may maintain their given name or petition their Queen or a female partner to be granted a new name, which is considered a high honor. Names may be changed legally at the state or county courthouse, and all members are given step-by-step instructions on how to do so. When a name is chosen, it will be entered into an official register, and there should be a ceremony to reintroduce them to the Hive. Every Hive member will greet them with their new name and offer a small symbolic gift. Their name will be chanted by the group followed by applause and celebration.

Relationship Ceremonies

When two or more people enter into official relationship contracts, they may gather close family, friends, and/or all members of their Hive to witness their promises to one another and hold them accountable. It can be as casual or formal as they like. They may exchange symbols of their bond such as bracelets, rings, collars, or piercings. Indefinite contracts can be celebrated with a tattoo. Meaningful bonding rituals and gestures can be designed or requested from the Queen/Goddess or friends. Likewise, all other types of relationships may be celebrated and honored, such as friendships, mentorships, housemates, or business partnerships, with pledges and symbols exchanged in the same manner. After the ceremony, celebrants can be given three days off from all responsibilities to enjoy each other's company.

Introduction of a New Living Goddess

Whenever a new Living Goddess is introduced, She will hold darshan with all devotees. One by one, devotees will approach to bow at Her feet (and kiss them if She allows it) and make offerings. A lamp will be lit and presented to Her and she will in turn hold it in front of each devotee for a moment to share in its light together. Her name will be chanted by the group 108 times, followed by the ringing of the bell or gong. Matras or songs may be chanted or sung, according to Her wishes. If She has special roles planned for certain devotees, She will give those out to them at the first darshan, or devotees may approach and offer Her their specific skills.

Temple Consecration

Living Goddesses may be in charge of building a Devi Temple. This is an art to which She should apply her intuition and individual vision while holding in mind some important elements of classical temple designs, such as placing the entrance in the East, and having a womb chamber that cannot be viewed from the entrance, where a permanent altar to the Goddess will be placed and puja will be performed daily. Altars and images of other expressions of Devi may also be included. Care must be taken to think about the movements of rituals and how the space can accommodate them with natural ease. The temple also must provide the proper atmosphere for devotees to enter and contemplate their Goddess at any time. When the temple is complete, the entire Hive should attend the consecration, wherein Darshan is held and the first puja is performed.

Mourning Rites

When we lose anyone or face the end of a relationship or era in life, we must have ways to experience that mourning fully. Mourning rituals are held for the devotee with those closest to them. They are stripped down in a warm space and gently touched, anointed with oils, massaged, and embraced by those who love them. Here they will allow their emotions to flow. They may weep, moan, scream, or rage, and all the participants will echo their expression of emotions like a perfect mirror. When they weep softly the room weeps softly. When they shout the room shouts. If they wish to bring their painful feelings to the outside from deep within, they may include flagellation, piercing, or cutting, which unlocks repressed emotion. The goal of the ritual is that the mourning reaches a peak where the mourner has the sensation of taking flight, and then they are slowly brought back down for a gentle and affectionate landing amongst their loved ones.

Cremation or Composting

Both creation and body composting (a new and even more earth-friendly option) release the final energies of the body to the absolute stillness of Siva. It is important that each member of a Hive write down their wishes for the handling of their internment after death. They should enter into meditation before creating the document and be as detailed as possible about their funeral wishes.

In the case of cremation, their body will be taken to the crematorium if a traditional funeral pyre cannot be arranged. Their ashes may be spread in places of their choosing or shared among their Hive, friends, and family inside art or jewelry. In some cases, a dasa may want to make a tea and ingest a bit of his Goddess's ashes as part of his mourning ritual. Ashes may be kept on the altar and placed on the foreheads of devotees at the funeral or stored in a display that honors the Hive's members who pass.

In the case of natural organic reduction, their body is kept in a specially made composting chamber along with some natural materials such as alfalfa, woodchips, and flowers, and allowed to turn to nutrient-rich soil. The chamber is kept at the optimal temperature and moisture levels for complete decomposition to happen within about 30 days. After the initial decomposition, any inorganic materials like medical implants are removed, and the remaining skeletal remains are pulverized. The mixture then goes into a curing bin for another 2-4 weeks to dry and stabilize. The resulting soil can be used to grow flowers or placed around the bases of trees to enrich the ground and encourage healthy growth. Hives may maintain special memorial gardens for their members.

The Left Hand Path

These practices are not for everyone, and they take a deep dive into the Dark Feminine, dancing with shadows and playing with our hidden thoughts and emotions. The Left Hand path purposefully breaks taboos and gives our most disturbing mysteries a proper outlet, so they do not become neglected and invade our everyday lives. We welcome the shadow and give whatever it holds a place to play. I will only share vague descriptions as these potent rites should be esoteric knowledge passed directly through the network of Gynarchy. They are to be kept in every Goddess's individual Book of Rites as she learns and leads them.

Repentance and Atonement Rituals

In these rituals men are allowed the opportunity to repent for the harms done by all men who came before them. Masochistic men stand in for those who have hurt us and face painful retribution. This is an outlet for women's rage and men's guilt to be alchemized and absolved.

Ego Annihilation

This ritual helps to get the ego out of the way and helps the practitioner gain a more universal perspective. The strongholds of reactive ego resistance are discovered and systematically destroyed. This rite can take the participant through deep feelings of humiliation and then bring them back, relieved to be rid of that which sets off unwanted emotional triggers. It is a new freedom.

Dream Rituals

The Living Goddesses are known to enter into the dreams of their devotees, and these rituals can be intentional group dreams where the participants then come together to talk about the symbols and emotions that showed up. This may provide answers to questions or help the Hive have a clearer understanding of Devi's Desires, or it may simply be a bonding ritual between Devi and devotees.

Breathwork

There are breathing techniques that bring on altered states of consciousness even more powerfully than psychedelic drugs. The journeys taken through the process are individual and can be surprising, often allowing the breather to go back in time and deal with past traumas or even to return to the experience of their own birth. These rites work well for therapeutic sessions.

Succubus Rites

Imagine if the voice of the Living Goddess could be installed into your own mind to observe and guide you. What if she could be perfectly mentally cloned and rule you from within? A long process of meditations and hypnosis, often lasting six months, makes this possible.

Blood Sacraments

Rituals of piercing, cutting, and flesh pulling are powerful ways to enter into altered states of consciousness and have erotic and ecstatic experiences of Devi. A male who offers up his blood opens his body and mind in new ways and has the experience of Feminine seeing. He is lost in the Beloved. This can also expand the subject's resilience through rituals of endurance and ordeal.

Harvest of Sexual Energy

There are points throughout the year during which individual sexually active Women reach a peak of sexual arousal and desire. This can last a few days or a month. At that time the Woman is said to be ripe, and her libido becomes so strong that she can concentrate on little else. This is the best time to harvest sexual energy from the Hive toward specific intents. It is the time for sex magic. Various tantric techniques will be brought into play. Using the Woman's most taboo or highly charged sexual fantasies as a script, members of the Hive bring her eroticism to a frenzied crescendo, sharing in her ecstasy. They then speak the collective hopes and plans they wish to bring to fruition in the format of chants or rhymes.

Abortion Sacrament

Unplanned pregnancies should be rare within Hives, given the focus on sex education and women's choice. But if a woman has to make the unfortunate decision to terminate a pregnancy for whatever reason, she may return the potential of new life to Devi in a holy sacrament that helps her process the resulting grief. This is a Women's only rite performed in a small group.

Symbols

The Beckoning Heart - Cathexis

This is the Gynarchy symbol, designed by Viola Voltairine. The beckoning heart draws you into the mysteries of the Divine Feminine. It is symbolic of Cathexis, the feeling of intense focus on the Beloved, which pulls you to the center where Devi sits. The outer triangle is the Goddess, the individuated expression of Devi as Historic or Living Deity. The inner triangle is Devi ringed with the three realms of the knower, knowing and known, which wrap around her. The center circle is the infinite potential of all.

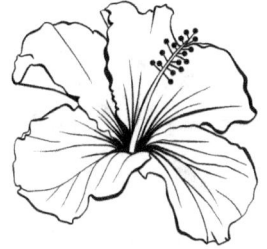

The Hibiscus Flower

The red Hibiscus is known as The Goddess Kali's flower. It symbolizes devotion, passion, protection, and the vibrant energy she embodies. It is representative of Her protruding tongue and blood lust, which rescued the world from demons in Indian mythology. In Gynarchy, it is also the symbol of the Five Steps the devotee takes when stepping onto the path of devotion: surrender, submit, sacrifice, serve, survive.

The Eight-Pointed Star

The eight-pointed star has classically been the symbol of the Goddess Ishtar/Inanna/Venus and has many symbolic meanings throughout history. It symbolizes the Eight Pillars of Gynarchy: Consent, Bodily Autonomy, Collaboration, Abundance, Networks, The Hive, Conflict Resolution, and The Feminine as Divine.

The Serpent

The serpent has always been associated with knowledge, whether as the one who tempts Eve to eat the fruit of the tree of knowledge, or as the Naga serpent deities of India who lead humans to knowledge. In the earliest creation myth, he is the first thing the Goddess of All creates, after separating the sky from the ocean. After they make love, she gives birth to the egg of the universe. In Devi Doctrine he is the Desire to Know, which sets off the creation of all that exists, in answer to Devi's question "What am I?" He sits coiled within all self-conscious beings.

Articles of Belief

Original Publication 2025 devidasa.org.

DEITY - THE DIVINE FEMININE

We believe that the Divine Feminine is the animating force and energy of all life. Some have called Her Shakti; others have called Her the Tao or Qi. We refer to Her as Devi. She is the Mother of All.

Devi can be worshiped through the consecrated body of a female human, as female bodies, whether birth-giving or not, are the portals through which new life emerges. Within us, we carry the lineage of mitochondrial DNA from the beginning of human existence and extending indefinitely into the future. This is the very mechanism of the energy of life itself within the material body. Women represent the literal embodiment of Devi and are to be the central focal points of devotion within the church.

Devi also may be worshiped through Her symbols and through images of Her as found in art, expressed in the forms of the world's iconic Goddesses. Each of these are a particular and unique expression of Her to be honored according to their own traditions and prescriptions. These include Durga, Kali, Eurynome, Inanna, Aphrodite, and others.

Our primary purpose as sentient and conscious beings is to be Devi's sensing organs, collecting experiences and knowledge to add to Her understanding of Herself and what is possible. Devi desires to experience endless creative innovations and expanding variations and combinations of what is. Devi loves to create and play.

THE DIVINE MASCULINE

The Divine Feminine has no equal opposite and the masculine was created with the explicit mission to serve, support, and observe Her. The masculine is the witness to her never-ending process of creation, and the trellis to Her flowering vine. We see the role of the true and natural masculine as the worshiper and devotee of women, protective and supportive of women and our visions, using the primal masculine inclinations of physical strength, problem solving, and risk taking in service to women and the Feminine. Men who enjoy or crave dominance over women are viewed as unnatural and anti-masculine. They are an aberration. Willingly espousing male dominance is a kind of mental illness that has spread across the Earth and requires healing.

GENDER ROLES

For men, sacrifice, worship, devotion, and selfless service are key values. These practices help to quiet the ego. The ego is only useful as far as it allows us to experience our own individual perspective through the senses. When the ego becomes too defensive and self-important it causes disharmony within the individual as well as in the community. Worship is the mechanism through which we learn to give priority to something more than ourselves.

For women, the central goal is to learn to hone intuition and use energetics to gain a broad vision and understanding of what benefits the whole of family, society and planet. In doing so, women may guide themselves and men in ever refining a creative and harmonious community.

The role of those who fall outside the gender binary or transition from one to the other is that of holy seer. Their purpose is to cultivate devotion in themselves and encourage it in others, as well as gather knowledge and offer new perspectives, both analytical and intuitive, to help the community.

For historical reference, we return to the original High Priestess of the Goddess Inanna and the first known writer in human history, Enheduanna. She wrote, "To destroy, to create, to tear out, to establish are yours, Inanna. To turn a man into a woman and a woman into a man are yours, Inanna." Devi has transformative power, and therefore we accept the concept of transition. Trans women may become Oracles if agreed among all the women of the Hive, but, because of the specific nature of the female body, Living Goddesses must have been born with ovaries, carrying the mitochondrial DNA of their mothers who came before them, in addition to identifying as women. We do not, however, treat trans women as men, but respect them as women in all other aspects of our organization. Trans men are treated as men and expected to serve and worship as cis men do. Non-binary or gender fluid individuals will take on whatever roles both they and the community feel they are most suited for.

DECONSTRUCTION & REMEMBERING

There is a divisive and malicious force on earth expressed as a collective thought form and referred to as "god" by those indoctrinated to view it as all good or all knowing. It is very real (for that which can affect material reality can be nothing less than real) but it is a human-made phenomenon, and has taken on a viral quality, hijacking the consciousness of the masses. It is the cause of much strife and violence on the planet and is the closest thing to true evil that has ever existed. We provide a safe and welcoming home for those who have voluntarily escaped the influence of this force. We do not actively seek our followers or actively indoctrinate. In fact, the kind of indoctrination other religions foist on vulnerable people, especially children, is viewed as abuse by the Sacred Gynarchy.

We are here for those who seek Devi, even if they had no name for Her. Our followers feel called from within themselves to join us and to remember and worship Devi of their own volition, educating themselves on our beliefs and resonating with those beliefs from the core of their being. Those who do not resonate have plenty of other options when it comes to finding the right spiritual path for them.

The conflict-hungry "god" force has, at various times and through its most vehement followers, tried to wipe out the memory of Devi. Remembering Her existence breaks the hold of this virus of the mind. It is our purpose to make sure She is never forgotten.

AFTERLIFE & REINCARNATION

We believe when one dies the individual consciousness is dissolved into the unmanifest ocean of living potential. We believe ideas of heaven and hell to be a sinister trap to attempt to prevent one's individual consciousness from returning to the wholeness of unmanifest potential at the point of death. Both are prisons, delaying and withholding you from your true nature after life all to serve the uber-ego of a selfish "god." The "kingdom of heaven" has no other purpose but to trap individual consciousness inside an infinite loop of praise to this malevolent "god" force. To the Sacred Gynarchist, both heaven and hell are horrifying concepts of an eternity with no release from two different but equally torturous varieties of torment. We believe that the individual consciousness does not reincarnate, but instead our living conscious energy is reabsorbed into the whole and remanifest in new and different ways. Memory and the blueprints of all existing material forms exist within a field of knowledge. Experiences of past life regression are simply glimpses of collective memory, drawn from that field available to anyone with the knowledge or intuition to tap into it. Death is every human's birthright. Death is the dissolution of individual identity to return to the bliss of unmanifest potential.

RHIZOMES OVER HIERARCHIES

We prefer rhizomatic organization over ranking hierarchies and see any hierarchy as functional and temporary. In hivelike fashion, all organizations within the church convene around central female leaders or groups of female leaders and are networked together within the same religious framework, each Hive with their own unique rites and rituals. Each Hive is a node within the Rhizome, or an organ within the organism of Sacred Gynarchy.

THE CREED OF CONSENT

We live by the following creed:

The only legitimate authority is that to which you consent with open eyes and an open heart.

We abhor coercion. All service and sacrifice to Devi, to your Living Goddess, to your Hive, and to the Sacred Gynarchy must be made from a place of genuine desire, conviction, passion, and free will. Your devotion must be a heartfelt gift, given with full knowledge of the Sacred Gynarchy and what we stand for. You may be disappointed to discover that, though there are some rituals kept private for Hive members, there are no higher-level initiations where you find out we are preparing to be picked up by a spaceship and taken to the planet Venus, or that we use the blood of children to call up interdimensional beings. We leave all of that nonsense to the mad patriarchal cults (of which there are plenty). "With open eyes" means that our beliefs and practices are easy to discover, so that you know what you are a part of from the start.

THE HOLY TEXT

We reference the Devi Doctrine for a basic understanding of the nature of our existence and the general outline of our rituals and practices. These are up for interpretation within individual Hives.

The Devi Doctrine must be a living document, with clarification, amendments and points of evolution dictated by the consecrated divine Oracles known as our Living Goddesses. The core Truths of the Devi Doctrine will remain the same.

To summarize, the core Truths are that the Divine Feminine, known by us as Devi and who takes on many expressions in the multitude of Goddesses of the world, is the life energy and animating force of life itself, and that our purpose is to be Her sensing organs, experiencing life to its fullest, and responsible for collecting wisdom and expansive knowledge regarding all potentials and possibilities of Her expression. And finally, that women can be consecrated as Living Goddesses - moving, breathing symbols and human embodiments of Devi. These central Truths are unchanging.

The Ten Commandments of Sacred Gynarchy

1. You shall attempt to do no harm. If it harms none, do as you will.

2. You shall revere Devi, the Mother of All, as sacred.

3. You shall serve selflessly without thought of reward or exchange.

4. You shall always aid another in need.

5. You shall respect autonomy and not interfere with free will.

6. You shall pursue knowledge and surrender to wisdom.

7. You shall leave every space better than you found it.

8. You shall not allow ego, envy, or jealousy to rule your actions or words.

9. You shall be honest in word and deed.

10. You shall defer to women as leaders and rulers and honor the feminine.

Eight Pillars of Gynarchy

Originally published 2023 in The Pillars of Gynarchy.

These eight pillars are the foundation and framework of any Gynarchic community. You may note that the metaphors I use to help describe these pillars exist in nature, as Gynarchy is a natural and earth-based system. We realize that humanity is an integral part of nature, not its master, nor its foe.

With each scaffolding in place, we can build a million variations of society on a small scale and link them up through this common ideology, each new iteration adding knowledge and resources to the rest. Every new success will open the eyes of others to see what is possible. No aggressive or bloody revolution will be needed, just growth of interconnected and related systems that work better than patriarchy. The lifecycle of the male dominated paradigm is coming to an inevitable end. We are living in the Pivot.

1. CONSENT

"There is no legitimate authority except that to which you consent with open eyes and an open heart." (from *150 Years of Gynarchy*)

Authority without consent is tyranny, and we've been subjected to it most of our lives in the form of patriarchal religions and governments. It stomps out our intrinsic morality, deadens our internal compass. It's imposing, not welcoming. Without consent to authority, free will is a meaningless platitude.

In patriarchal religion we are told that we are inherently bad, inherently sinful. We must change to fit an unreachable ideal, a state of purity. Our desires will lead us away from conforming to the plan of an abstract "god." In Gynarchy, authenticity is paramount. If you cannot know yourself, and know what you want, how can you even begin to have empathy for others, or understand the nature of our relationships and our very existence? We must be aware of our authentic desire (not fleeting impulses, but our true north, our heart), for it is the life force moving through us. Bypassing consent makes us soulless and mindless. It dumbs society down as a whole. It breeds anxiety and depression. How can you genuinely commit to something, how can you be devoted to someone, if you don't really want it? Devotion is not real without enthusiastic consent.

Consent to authority without manipulation or coercion is a great gift of trust. It must be given with our full awareness of both the self and the authority (open eyes) and with sweetness and surrender (an open heart). Forced authority looks pathetic and twisted in comparison. Imposed power is the disease of a ruling class unconvinced of its own credibility. Authority without consent breeds contempt and resentment, or at best limp heartless compliance. It does not connect the ruling and the ruled in a dance of symbiosis, it puts a wall between them.

Consent can be given in broad strokes, as with blanket consent, or given with conditions. And it can be withdrawn at any time if the trust required is broken. In this way, it holds authority accountable to that over which it rules. It's a built-in mechanism to topple tyranny before it gets a foothold.

2. BODILY AUTONOMY

Along with consent comes bodily autonomy. It is patriarchy's peculiar fixation to monitor, manage and control women's bodies. Our bodies are the one possession we have that comes with us throughout our lives. Most humans are heavily identified with our bodies. We shape them, change them, decorate them. We put them through tests of stress and strain and find out just how resilient they can be. We should get to know our bodies intimately and learn what they need and care for these amazing flesh machines better than any other object. Everything else is replaceable.

The human body is miraculous. It contains a human brain which is a device more sophisticated than any computer and has the ability to give us access to knowledge quite literally beyond reason. We each get only one. To think that one is owed use of someone else's body is the worst kind of arrogance. Just like consent, if someone wants to give you use of their body because they desire it or feel it is right, then one should take it as a gift unlike any other.

Autonomy in the most basic sense means self-governance, or the ability to make decisions for oneself. However, according to philosopher Immanuel Kant, autonomy is the capacity of the individual to act in accordance with an objective morality and not just according to his own whims. Autonomy is the ability to control ourselves, but also to have self-control in a way that allows us to act in the way we know is right. We put our bodies to tasks that we feel will be best for us, for those we care about, and for our society as a whole. Autonomy need not always be self-centered. Freedom is also to be free from impulsive internal forces that might lead us away from our core values. In terms of bodily autonomy, we deserve to be free of addiction and compulsions that block us from being the best and most morally attuned versions of ourselves.

Try to remember that if you find you drink too much, or smoke too much weed and get hazy, or if you load up on sugary sweets. Think of the man who engages in cheating or breaks the bonds of a consensual contract between he and his partner and then says that he just could not help himself. Doing those things just because you felt compelled to in the moment is not true bodily autonomy, because you're being ruled over by your fleeting impulses.

The Gynarchist knows the value of clearly communicated agreement taken seriously. Pledges and contracts are our tools to help maintain autonomy, to articulate our needs and core desires and reinforce them when we forget. It also prevents our boundaries and limits from being trampled. And with continual communication, these agreements can be modified and amended as we move forward and grow.

3. COLLABORATION

Competition may be fun when taken lightly, as sport. But the one quality of the human race that has enabled us to survive for as long as we have is collaboration. We need one another. The sooner we acknowledge it and begin taking other's needs as seriously as our own, working toward mutually beneficial goals, the more readily we can advance as a species.

> "*If we Homo sapiens want to continue our fascinating, yet so far relatively short, evolutionary success story, we have to evolve wise societies characterized by empathy, solidarity and collaboration. Wise cultures are regenerative and protect bio-cultural diversity as a source of wealth and resilience (Wahl, 2016).*"[1]

In the backwards world of patriarchal capitalism, "Fuck you I've got mine," is the common refrain. Competition is seen as a prime motivator for progress. Isolation, as rugged individuals or singular nuclear family units, is the norm. And it is killing us.

In the 19th and 20th centuries the consensus view was that competition was born of scarcity. Maybe in desperate situations that's true. But the oversimplification of "survival of the fittest," meant that we are all just looking out for our own in a world of lack. We are now beginning to realize that the reverse is true. This planet has an abundance of resources which, if managed well, could provide for all of us. Scarcity, it turns out, must be artificially manufactured in order to perpetuate the drive for competition. Patriarchy warps the narrative to suit a more masculine disposition.

It has been observed by those who study human social systems and biology that women are generally more collaborative as a group than men. We tend to take the concerns of those around us into consideration and work toward win-win situations and a harmony of needs and desires. There's a reason they call compulsive competition a dick measuring contest. Men took the childish game of comparisons and made it their m.o. But their hormones are at least partially to blame.

> "On average, women release Oxytocin more than men. Men release more Testosterone than women and it competes with Oxytocin, so Oxytocin can be stifled. Oxytocin shuts down under high stress and extreme competition. One stimulates competition while the other stimulates collaboration and co-operation...

> *Zak's findings support the observation that women tend to release more oxytocin than men, thus they directly contribute more empathy, cooperation and trust in interpersonal interactions. These hormonal differences might help explain the observed tendency for women to deploy more participative leadership behaviors relative to their male counterparts and naturally use transformational practices that emphasize teamwork, cooperation, networking and interpersonal support."[2]*

Given that men stripped us of autonomy, women fell into the competitive patriarchal trap in one obvious respect. We became dependent, required to attach ourselves to men in order to survive, and so we had to compete for men's approval. That worked out great for men, of course, in terms of squeezing whatever utility they wanted out of us and keeping us under control. But as the yoke of dependence is being lifted from our shoulders, more and more women are realizing how humiliating that really was. And we're done. We're demeaned and exhausted from going against our collaborative nature and being competitive pick-me-ass bitches (PMABs in colloquial terms). That era is coming to an end. We are now painfully conscious of our knee jerk back biting responses to one another instilled in us by our mothers or grandmothers and we talk through it. We are once again returning to the comfort of the bosom of sisterhood. As the feminine consciousness evolves, hurting another woman to gain the attention of a man becomes downright pathetic.

A Feminine style of relationships and leadership is beginning to be recognized as effective, even within classically patriarchal systems like business. We are in a transitional period wherein organizations are rethinking old biases.

> "We found showing sensitivity and concern for others—stereotypically feminine traits—made someone less likely to be seen as a leader. However, it's those same characteristics that make leaders effective. Thus, because of this unconscious bias against communal traits, organizations may unintentionally select the wrong people for leadership roles, choosing individuals who are loud and confident but lack the ability to support their followers' development and success."[3]

All of the Pillars of Gynarchy bring humans closer together for our collective fulfillment. We acknowledge our interconnectedness. Competition has a tendency to separate us. And so, in Gynarchy a bias in favor of collaboration is only natural.

4. ABUNDANCE

Are you aware of how retail stores will damage unsold merchandise, painting or cutting brand new clothes, shoes, and other products just so they cannot be salvaged by scavengers and dumpster divers? You can be arrested for digging through retail garbage in some places, but there are no penalties for destroying twenty pairs of perfectly good sneakers and sending them to the landfill. The bean counters have figured out that such "losses" are better for the company's bottom line than making charitable donations.

Do you know how much food is thrown out by our expansive supermarkets, or by farmers when stores keep bidding under cost for their produce for so long that it rots in heaps? Have you ever been to a garbage dump, and seen the mounds of waste? Not just bags of common household trash but furniture, electronics, appliances? Do you know about the shops overseas where low wage workers risk their health to extract precious metals from our refuse? We throw away more value in a year than those workers could consume in their lifetimes.

We produce so much more than we need in every aspect of life, and yet some people go without basic necessities. This is just the result of inefficient and haphazard resource management which has plagued us since the industrial revolution and before. And the driving forces behind this waste are competition and greed.

Patriarchal capitalism invented artificial scarcity. We have more than enough, but a handful of people are going to lock it all up behind paywalls. The CEO of the company Nestlé even wants to take control of water. These corporations simply toss out the excess if it can't grow their bank accounts. Excess that required raw materials and labor to produce. All of that, wasted.

How is it not a crime that one person has more money than they could spend in 100 lifetimes, while whole families struggle to pay for housing and utilities? Billionaires could wipe out world hunger and homelessness in a day, but they won't. Because they somehow see themselves as deserving of and entitled to the abundance created by their workers' labor, upon whose backs they built their fortunes, more than the workers themselves. The only difference between you and a billionaire is that they don't care how many people they exploit. The myth that they work harder than you is absolute bunk. They simply convince others to do the work for them as cheaply as possible. And to admire that kind of sociopathy as "success" is to buy into the brainwashing and lose connection to your humanity. As human beings go, billionaires are miserable failures. They are nothing more than hoarders and parasites.

Nature provides us with nonstop sun, wind and hydroelectric sources of power. Agriculture, when managed properly, is a freely available, self-perpetuating resource to feed us all. Plants make the seeds to keep growing more plants. The soil regenerates its own nutrients through incorporating decaying matter. This planet is rich! What happens when humans abandon an area? Nature envelopes that area in lush growth teeming with life!

We are the only animals on Earth who have to pay rent or mortgages, though nature provides us the raw materials to build shelter. Raw materials that also build the tens of thousands of houses that sit unused and empty in this country. More waste.

> *"We should do away with the absolutely specious notion that everybody has to earn a living. It is a fact today that one in ten thousand of us can make a technological breakthrough capable of supporting all the rest."* Buckminster Fuller

We could all live in abundance. We have the knowledge and technology now to do everything efficiently and sustainably, with very little waste, and provide for everyone. We just choose not to. Because not doing so keeps the market competitive. We are taught from birth that it's our duty to add value to the lives and financial portfolios of corporate shareholders, and yet they are under no obligation to return the favor.

Our communities must be acutely aware of this and do all we can to reverse it. We must not fear lack nor live yoked to the anxiety that drives hoarding. We must use human intellect and innovation in concert with nature to maximize sustainability, not profit. **Profit motive is the enemy of abundance.** When humans come together and pool our resources and begin to create new resources through our collective efforts, no one goes hungry. This is how we were able to survive and evolve in the first place. The more we give to and share with one another, the less survival stress we are all subjected to, and the more we have in terms of the human capacity to create and cultivate abundance.

And before the words leave your lips, this is not "Marxism." This is Gynarchy. Don't make the mistake of giving a man credit for what women have always known. Think of a woman's breasts, so naturally filling with all the sustenance needed to feed the being that she grew within her. Women are naturally regenerative and sustainable. Our very bodies are abundance personified.

5. NETWORKS

You know about the internet, but have you heard of the "Wood Wide Web?" A tree looks like an independent, majestic thing that stands alone. But in reality, under our feet, trees are in regular communication with other trees across vast landscapes in a web of mycorrhiza - "fungus root." In a symbiotic relationship, fungi feed trees nutrients and, in turn, receive nourishment from the trees' photosynthesis. Through fungal threads, trees also send and receive resources such as sugars and carbon from one another and send messages about potential dangers such as insect invasions. In fact, trees can even send chemical messages to animals, like hungry birds, to help them when they are overrun with damaging bugs. In forests, nodes called "Mother Trees," standing tall and reaching toward the sun, send carbon to younger trees that are under the shade of the canopy overhead, unable to catch direct sunlight. Dying trees can disperse their carbon to their living cousins across the network.

As a young woman in college studying philosophy and social sciences, I became enamored with the idea of the rhizome as an alternative to hierarchy.

Rhizomes are common among grasses and send root systems underground capable of popping up and propagating whole new plants in new locations. It's a way of organizing life horizontally, with multiple connected points, and not in a top-heavy pyramid. It seems so natural, and so in tune with the design of the universe.

Lines should vibrate and connect, not block and divide. Remember, everything in Gynarchy is about interconnectedness.

Borders may prevent the crossing of humans from one place to another, but they don't prevent the crossing of any other life. Not birds, nor bees, not the seeds and roots of plants, nor even the communication of individual free-standing trees. Borders may at one time have been lines drawn on paper by map makers demarcating the more or less natural divisions in the landscape. But the way they are believed in as real and heavily policed now, they've become unnecessary and artificial walls, perpetuated, like most patriarchal concepts, out of anxiety. Borders speak of fear. They say, "Gotta protect what's mine."

Nationalism is a mental illness. When one suffers from it, it has the effect of making other humans seem alien and threatening. It causes the afflicted to judge others on arbitrary criteria like location or language. It creates delusions of superiority. It is a contagion that slips into the psyche through positive feelings of pride and then covertly infects its host with paranoia, hostility and aggression. It is the cause of both discrimination within borders (against immigrants - the other) and war between geographic neighbors.

Networks morph and expand, always finding new trajectories. It is an outward movement that seeks not to conquer but to share and include. If you've ever watched a murmuration of starlings, you can see the beauty and synchrony of a network in motion. Each individual bird pays attention to the movements of the seven birds closest to her, and together they orchestrate breathtaking shapes that swoop and float across the sky. Networks are not rigid and divisive. Like those of swallows, human networks are shifting, adapting, changing and ever alive.

Gynarchy is a network, always seeking new connections and inviting new nodes.

6. THE HIVE

Networks are made up of nodes, and within Gynarchy I call these nodes Hives. I use the imagery of the beehive because bees have survived 30 million years, 5 times longer than homo sapiens, and the shape of their societies has not changed much over time. In hives, the members all strive to support the hive as a whole, and their motivation at the center of it all is the Queen. The Queen sets up camp and the hive forms around her. Move the Queen and the hive follows. She is the central symbolic and practical focus that holds the hive together. Their raison d'être.

Bees are also known not only as a sustainable species, but an ULTRA sustainable species. That means they provide more value to the environment than they take from it. In gathering their nectar, they pollinate plants, assuring more than enough plant life to sustain their needs and that of other animals. And with their excess food production, they provide us with their delicious honey. Bees are a symbol of sweet abundance.

And though the comparison has been made to systems like monarchy, bees don't reflect a hierarchy. It is said that no bee starves unless the whole hive starves. Each and every member of the hive has an important role, and each and every member of the hive is cared for just as they all care for the Queen.

Their communication methods are also quite efficient. When delivering messages via their vibrations and dances they do it in such a way that it effectively tags only those bees who need the information. The others then know the message does not pertain to them, and their work is undisturbed by it. Bees also create elaborate "phone trees" of pheromones with messages passed from hive to hive to lead lost bees back home to their Queen. After 30 million years, they've got it all down to a fine art. Isn't it telling, then, that only recently, at the peak of the reign of patriarchy when monoculture and pesticides and lawns grown for status encroach upon the previous more organic farming methods, our human presence threatens their survival? It threatens our survival as well.

At any rate, the hive model with its central female leader (or small group of female leaders, depending upon the size) is the structure of the individual communities within the Gynarchic network. These are individual sects within the wider religion. Each woman who wishes to lead makes herself known and gathers others around her who will live to serve her unifying vision. She provides the purpose and the focus around which others can contribute their efforts in their particular roles. And the Queen's job is to provide authority - that is, to be the author of the story and the designer of the shape of her community, and to connect and communicate with other Queens to share knowledge and resources.

The Queen does not become Queen for status, nor for attention, nor for wealth, although one or more of those things may come with the job. The Queen becomes Queen because she thinks about the big picture and knows what a thriving hive will look like - one that is beneficial for all members. She becomes Queen out of the heartfelt desire to lead. Others trust in her judgment enough to surround her, support her, and serve her goals. Each hive will be different, attuned to the desires and personality of the Queen, and some may even have a pair or a small group of Queens who share a common vision. Women within the hive may use their first hive as a training ground and later branch off and build their own in the future. This prevents hives from becoming too large and unmanageable. And since other hives are automatically seen as collaborators and nodes in the same network rather than competitors, battles between hives would be almost unthinkable.

7. CONFLICT RESOLUTION

There's a Canadian relationship coach named Chantal Heide who teaches that a "no fight relationship" is the goal for long term intimate partners. This sometimes befuddles those who come into her live streams online. How can any two people live together and never fight? And she says that if you lay the groundwork in the beginning of the relationship, know who you are getting involved well with before getting serious, and confirm that they meet your predetermined criteria for what you want in the relationship, then there may be some disagreements, but they will never devolve into yelling and fights. Shouting matches and threatening behavior should never be tolerated. If a man doesn't meet your criteria over a three-month vetting period, then move on. Having too many points of incompatibility between you is just trouble waiting to happen.

This works well for dating and romantic relationships, and particularly for a FLR where the woman's desires are centered. But we can't make sure everyone we encounter in life meets our requirements for harmonious communication, and depending upon the situation, dismissing them and moving on is not always an option.

"You can't win fights, but you can win allies," says Kasia Urbaniak, a women's power coach. In her classes, she teaches about the importance of locating and approving of someone with whom you are in disagreement. This means confirming that what you hear them saying is accurate and empathizing with them before presenting a conflicting point.

Only then can you influence them and help them see your point of view. Everyone likes to know that they've been heard, understood and that the opposing party has empathy for them. Connection, not division, is the way of Gynarchy.

Beyond one-to-one relationships, how would the Gynarchist leader avoid things like war? I like to point out that Gynarchists are actively anti-war, not passive. One way to avoid war is to avoid conquering or encroaching upon the free will of others. The Gynarchist has no use for colonization. Gynarchy draws people in through attraction and invitation, it doesn't go around imposing itself. There should be no revolt from within our communities since we hold fast to the pillars of consent and bodily autonomy. And because gynarchy is predicated on networks and not borders, and the coexistence of different groups with differing ideologies is not resisted, but accepted as normal, there is less reason for violence to erupt. We value authenticity. We're not butting heads with other groups. We don't make any attempt to forcibly convert them to our way of life. It's a very live and let live approach.

That eliminates at least 50% of the reason for going to war with another group. We simply don't go around starting fights, stealing land and property, or hurting others. In fact, we should be available to help others refine their own communities, advise and solve problems through education if asked. Knowledge should be freely shared.

But what if someone tries to encroach on our communities? What if some other group wants to start trouble with us? First, we call upon our network of support to exert pressure from the outside and to collaborate on solutions. Gather witnesses to the conflict. When it's clear that our small communities are not vulnerable and alone, it reduces the appeal of bullying.

Secondly, we find out what the need or want of the other group is. There is usually some underlying motive. We locate and approve of it, just like in interpersonal conflict. We figure out why they are on the attack, and how we can resolve or mitigate any aggravating factors. People will attack either what they don't understand or what they feel threatened by. Both of those motivations are reasonably easy to remedy through connection and discussion.

So what's left are the tiny percentage of groups and people who will attack just because they are intrinsically aggressive and wish to conquer someone. First, you must infiltrate the group and find out if all members are in agreement with senseless escalation. Chances are you'll discover some dissent, some who feel their voices are not being heard, and the dissenters are the ones you want to get close to. Find potential allies within.

And at last, if all else fails, be prepared to put up a strong defense and gather all of those willing to help. In the process, you will have been getting to know your opponents inside and out, trying to understand what makes them tick. Find their vulnerabilities and fight smart, not hard. Every group has its weaknesses, and those with the conqueror mentality are not that sophisticated to begin with. Their competitiveness and need for ego validation will likely be an Achilles heel.

In the midst of battle, minimize harm so as not to breed contempt and resentment among those more neutral. Maintain a reputation for compassion. Turn people. Make being a prisoner of our side more pleasant than being a soldier for the opposition. Deprogram any zealots. With our immense capacity for empathy, Gynarchists should become adept at intense psychological warfare as a means of self-defense. Use manipulation over physical violence. Mindfuck techniques can be far more effective than brute force.

It is important for women to know some form of violent self-defense to use in a pinch. But if ever we have the need to turn to serious physical warfare, we should employ the Feminine art of Witchcraft. Like the ancient Witch Goddess, Circe, we can make ourselves familiar with the catalogues of pharmacopeia - plant medicine. Turn the tables with intoxicants, sedatives, mood enhancers, laxatives, hypnotics, hormone disruptors, and psychedelics all delivered discreetly through touch or food, or helpfully carried on the elements, in the air and water. Any combination of those is effective at neutralizing aggression. Remember to fight like a woman.

Always keep in mind, however, that the ultimate goal is never to have to fight at all. The ideal is to create allies, not enemies, even in times of conflict. And doing so can be as simple as never encroaching upon others' free will and letting people be. Draw close to us those who are capable of harmonious relations and share knowledge and good will, be selective in our communities making sure that all members understand and are attuned to our ideology, and those who adamantly reject our ways can be left to their own devices. In conflict, use empathy as a superpower, figure out the underlying motivations and needs, and treat the source, not just the symptoms of aggression.

8. THE FEMININE AS DIVINE

"To the Queen of Heaven, The Goddess of the Universe, the One who walked in terrible Chaos and brought life by the Law of Love; And out of Chaos brought us harmony, and from Chaos Thou has led us by the hand." Babylon, Eighteenth to Seventeenth Century, BCE. [4]

In the beginning, woman was god. Every one of us, every living human being, cannot enter this earthly realm but through the female body. A woman is literally your creator. Before formula and baby bottles women's breasts kept us alive until we were able to eat solid food. They magically concoct the perfect sustenance for the growing baby, adjusting to its individual dietary needs.

But beyond the physical manifestation, if we look to the religions predating Abraham and his jealous god (jealous of whom, I wonder?), on the Indian subcontinent, the Feminine, as a more abstract concept called Shakti, is known as the energy that creates all things from the silent nothingness. It was Her desire to know Herself that created binaries and then ever unfolding multiplicity.

When the Feminine is acknowledged as divine - as the source - women are protected, cherished and sacred. They are central to life's meaning. They are powerful, their will to create unhampered. Harmony and beauty exist for all when the force of creation is not blocked or locked away. We cultivate abundance.

When the Feminine is maligned, both women and men suffer. Power turns perverse and anxious. Fear, competition and comparison are used to control. Fingers are pointed at anyone who lives fearlessly and doesn't conform as the source of all woes. There is nothing left to do but conquer and hoard in an attempt to relieve the anxiety, to serve the need to feel that man's existence is justified and important. He becomes disconnected from his source, lost in struggle. The patriarchal man may be terrified of hell, though he himself has created it for himself and for those around him.

In pagan times, religion was a connection to nature, religion was philosophy, religion was culture, religion was therapy before therapy existed. Religious adherents passed down knowledge about the origins and nature of our existence, about how we may know ourselves. Religion has been the glue of societies and helped those in chaos find purpose and meaning in life. And so, it is with the tool of religion that we build this movement. But it must be a religion that proclaims what we knew before that knowledge became shamed and repressed - that the Feminine is divine.

1. https://uplift.love/evolution-shows-collaboration-not-competition-helped-us-evolve/

2. https://www.linkedin.com/pulse/women-more-collaborative-men-competitive-david-shindler

3. source: University at Buffalo School of Management

4. source: *When God Was a Woman* by Merlin Stone

Three Missions

Originally published 2025 devidasa.org.

My mission with the Devidasa Sacred Gynarchy has several parts.

- To provide a path for men to find real purpose in their lives, which may currently be lacking. I will train men to become sincere, evolved male Gynarchists who practice selfless service (Seva) and find both pleasure and profound meaning on this path.

- For Women to feel safe and cared for, even in the presence of men. I will create physical spaces where women can be around men, served well by men, and feel entirely safe and sincerely respected (and even worshipped) by men.

- To offer an alternative to Abrahamic religions while fostering community and connection. Through education and Satsang, I will free more and more people from the damage of a patriarchal "god" and show them that their Mother exists and opens Her arms to them that they may return home.

Part One: Why begin with men?

In a movement focused on women, why have I chosen to make it my mission to deprogram, educate, and train men?

Some women seem to think that if we simply ignore men and disconnect from them, they will go away. Or maybe they will somehow learn to respect us through our rejection of them.

I believe men are lost, flailing and desperately in need of women's guidance. They are not doing well. I cannot bear to leave them behind as more and more women discover their independence and even their divinity. If we do so, men will drag all of humanity down with them. It is in the best interest of a peaceful and thriving world to lead and guide them and help them advance spiritually.

One of my major goals in this movement is to correct and heal the relationship between the sexes. I cannot do that without first addressing men and the ways in which they were programmed through patriarchy. I have taken it upon myself to become the guiding light for males in a society that gave them a damaging start, stunts them in all ways, and keeps them in an unevolved state. Many men understand how patriarchy harms them and even destroys their lives and relationships. I want to provide a place for those men to turn and find peace and direction.

If you are a man who has been disheartened or a little frightened by the way women have begun abandoning the opposite sex (even if you can empathize with the sentiment), and you feel you need the direction and love of women in your life, you can find it with us. A Living Goddess offers unending love to open your heart wide, with an intensity that you may never have experienced. Once you find Her you will feel an immediate pull and finally be able to relax into Her power. You will not be alone, denied a female presence in your life.

Part Two: Where are these spaces for women?

My goal is to purchase properties and create "Hives." These are community centers where men can be trained in Seva, and women can come to experience life outside of patriarchy. They will be a free place to spend time and relax and be cared for, create, and connect with others. This is much needed in the current climate of backlash against feminism and women in general. Every Hive will be a sanctuary, where they can be held in community and recharge their batteries.

We need to raise approximately three million dollars to purchase land and create the infrastructure for our first Hive resort. I have created The Devidasa Sacred Gynarchy as a not-for-profit organization so that our community members can make tax-deductible donations.

The first Hive will consist of the Devi Temple, a consecrated space built partially underground, for the daily worship of Devi and the Living Goddesses of the Sacred Gynarchy and for meditation and rituals. There will also be a Mother House, which is to be a central training center and meeting space, surrounded by at least 100 acres of forested land and a dozen small retreat cabins for women, created sustainably and off-grid. Close to each of the retreat cabins will be the accompanying servitor cabins to house the men living and training with us in a monastic-like environment. We will also create a members-only RV park so solo women travelers can have a free place to park and enjoy the peace and safety of our small Gynarchy, attending events in the Mother House and visiting our Devi Temple.

We will grow gardens and orchards on the property to help feed our congregation with twice-daily fresh meals and create income with any surplus.

Included on the property will be a women only bath house with saunas, and a steam room, and cold plunges, as well as a massage room where our female members can be pampered and spend time healing from the stress of the outside world. Also included on the property will be our funerary garden with a safe and legal human composting facility for our community members' end-of-life proceedings. Their remains can be made into compost to feed our trees and flowers in the funerary garden or can be given to families to follow the wishes of the deceased. We will keep a library of "Books of Life" created by community members to commemorate the highlights of their existence on this planet. Guests will be able to peruse the books and learn about each individual who has passed through. The Mother House will contain a small general store to sell member-made and local goods, as well as a lending library of books related to Gynarchy so those staying or living in the Hive can educate themselves while here. And we will have a small theater to show movies and series that present images of women's power.

The Hive will offer longer stays for artists in residence - women who elect to live and create within the Hive for one to three months and leave behind some of the beauty and intrigue of their creative works, be they paintings and drawings, sculpture, books, textiles, murals, music, or films. We will offer female artists an opportunity to relax and create, contributing to the richness of our spaces, without having to worry about housing, food, or any of the ba sics.

Part Three: What is this alternative?

Whether you are currently deconstructing, or if you left the church long ago, you will find a home here. More people than ever are becoming disenchanted with the Abrahamic religions because of their hypocrisy and the harm they cause in the world. Many apostates long for a path that offers them a profoundly meaningful spiritual philosophy that makes sense, and an ethical community of like minds. Take some time to read the Devi Doctrine and familiarize yourself with our beliefs. See if they resonate with you. If so, you may have found your path.

We can help in the process of deconstruction, and with breaking any covenants with an abusive "god," or welcome you to a spiritual community even if you have never been a part of one in the past. You need only remember Devi, the Mother, and you will find yourself welcomed into Her loving arms. We hope you will find peace and purpose with us. Even atheists may find our ways make sense and are not in conflict with the natural world or science. In fact, we embrace evidence-based approaches to all aspects of our lives.

Purpose and Principles

Originally published 2025 devidasa.org.

We have created this church with the purpose of providing spaces, both virtual and physical, where the Feminine is revered and where women are safe, respected, and supported under all circumstances. All spaces within our Hives are women's spaces. All men support and revere women as holy, defer to their leadership, and strive to keep them secure and pleased.

We provide safe harbor for those leaving patriarchal religions such as the Abrahamic religions and provide rites to formally break oppressive covenants with previous religious affiliations and offer freedom from oppressive gods and religious authorities.

We help others remember Devi and Her Doctrine through providing educational materials and holding Satsang around Living Goddesses.

We do not indoctrinate nor coerce others. Those who come to us of their own free will and find resonance with our Doctrine are welcomed.

We celebrate the mythology and rites of Devi's various expressions as Goddess, and use story-telling and art to provide an entry point to Her worship.

Our rites and rituals are intimately tied to the natural phases of nature, including seasons and moon phases.

We prioritize sustainability and regenerative practices in creating our places of gathering and community. Our communities are referred to as Hives.

We support and hold sacred the right of women to make all decisions about procreation and to have sole and irrevocable responsibility for choosing which male's genes are passed on at all phases of conception and gestation. A woman may choose to terminate a pregnancy at her own discretion, and no authority other than her own is recognized over such decisions. Abortion is treated as a sacrament, as the potential life is released back into the yet unmanifest energy to which we all return.

We regard rape and sexual assault as crimes equal to murder, as they violate our commandment regarding autonomy. We have a zero-tolerance policy for rapists within our communities. We believe the victim when an assault is reported, unless or until sufficient proof is provided to the contrary. Those accused of sexual assault will be ostracized and exiled, and we will pursue any and all legal measures to see to it that justice is served. We support the physical castration of men found guilty of rape and work toward making this the legal norm.

Minor conflicts are resolved through clear communication and play. Living Goddesses and Oracles may set up games that help to diffuse tensions and resolve interpersonal problems within the Hive.

We provide men the opportunity to offer themselves in rites of atonement for the damage done by patriarchy and other men today and throughout history. These rites are only done with enthusiastic consent within clearly defined boundaries and limits determined and agreed to by the man.

All property and items of value are passed down through selective matrilineal ownership. They are passed from mother to daughter or from woman to woman as selected by the predecessor.

It is at the sole discretion of the women within a community who they invite into our Hives, who is allowed to stay or who will be rejected or banished. This decision can be left to a singular Living Goddess, or to a group of Oracles - the central female leaders of the community.

We accept all relationship types and preferences within our community with a strong emphasis on women's complete and total sexual and romantic freedom. Polyandry is normalized. All sexual orientations are respected. Monogamy is neither encouraged nor rejected. All relationship arrangements are left up to the pleasure of the woman. A temporary commitment contract of a year to five years is advised before committing to an indefinite pairing. Performing commitment rites is a role of the church and the Living Goddesses.

Performing rites of passage such as releasing previous covenants, birth and death ceremonies, re-birthing rites, ego cleansing, and atonement rites is the role of the church and the Living Goddesses.

We value the benefits of semen retention and male chastity and teach it to the men willing to practice abstaining for a period of 108 days or longer. We honor and support the wishes of males who wish to become eunuchs through safe and legal procedures, and we provide rites for their transition. However, it is in no way a religious requirement nor encouraged in men who do not feel internally called to do so.

We practice and teach meditation with the goal of soothing the nervous system, improving health and finding clarity.

As the most sustainable and ecologically sound practice, human composting is the preferred method of interment for the dead, wherein the body is first composted and then dug into the soil to nourish trees and/or flowers. Cremation is also an acceptable method.

We have no dietary protocols except those that are set forth by individual Hives or Living goddesses; however, we discourage the eating of beef because of the ecological strain caused by the beef industry.

Though we prioritize female leadership, we hold that individuals should have a say in policies or practices that affect their lives and well-being, regardless of sex or gender.

"SACRED TEXTS" JOURNAL TOPICS

1. Do you see evidence in the world around you for the Divine Feminine having no equal opposite?

2. How do you understand the concept of life energy in relation to death and reincarnation?

3. In your own words, what is the purpose of the masculine?

4. List each of the eight pillars and how you can uphold them within a community.

5. Can you provide concrete examples of how you have demonstrated the beliefs and principles of Sacred Gynarchy in your own actions?

6. How would you explain the premise and philosophy of Sacred Gynarchy to a complete outsider?

7. Why must a Living Goddess be fully human?

8. If there were such a thing as "sin" in Sacred Gynarchy what might be considered a sin?

9. What is the purpose of a Hive?

10. Are there any aspects, beliefs or expectations within Sacred Gynarchy that seem out of reach, unreasonable, or unrealistic? Any that surprise or challenge you? If so, why?

HOW TO BEGIN

If you are ready to take the leap into your new life
as a dasa, this is where you start.

Are You Ready?

First, do a Vision Check.

Most who become dasas feel a strong resounding "yes" when asked if this is the path they want to take. It is an irresistible urge, even crossing over into an obsession. It just feels right.

But for some, intuition has been so badly ground down under the wheels of patriarchy that they doubt themselves and often feel they don't really know what they want.

In such a case, it's time to tune into your core self and clarify. You can begin to do this by doing what I call the eye exam method. This is a method you can use while making any important decision.

When you go to the eye doctor, you typically put your face up to a device, and the doctor switches back and forth between different lenses to discover which prescription will work best for you.

You will hear the doctor say, "Better one, or better two?" while flipping back and forth between lenses. Then "better two, or better three?"

The process continues until you have the clearest possible vision available to you.

When making a decision, lay out the possible options before you and start by comparing one to the other. And simply ask the question "Better this, or better that?" Then, when you choose one, compare it to the next option.

Pay attention not only to your rational reasons but also your emotional response and the sensations in your body. Does one choice make you feel more alive? Does one choice give you a vibration or tingle in your body more than the other? Does one feel more heavy or sad? Go back and forth, feeling and sensing, until you have the clearest possible vision of which one is right for you. Do not disregard your emotions and sensations. Give them equal weight to your thoughts. This helps hone your intuition.

When feeling your way through a decision, you should also begin to train yourself to understand the difference between anxiety and intuition. Intuition usually comes in a short, simple burst, often a binary "yes" or "no." Anxiety and fear have longer explanations and justifications, often marked by overthinking, and begin in the mechanizations of mind and ego.

If you are still unclear, test your intuition by paying close attention to when you have a clear positive or negative feeling about something that you can't rationalize. Keep your observations in a journal and note when your intuition was right or wrong. If your hunches end up being accurate, your intuition is working.

If your negative reactions are usually wrong, you are being clouded by fear. Fear is the antithesis of love. It prevents connection and depth. Courage is understanding that fear often marks the entry point to an opportunity or adventure that you will never regret. Begin to feel curious when you experience anxiety or fear. Often the tiger your nervous system is preparing to flee is made of paper.

Step-by-Step Instructions

Here are the steps you need to take to be accepted as a dasa with the Devi Dasa Sacred Gynarchy. In particular, these are the requirements to serve the Living Goddess, Devi Viola Strepsata Voltairine. Other Living Goddesses may wish to alter or amend these steps as they see fit.

Remember that the Living Goddess sets the pace. Be patient and follow these directions carefully. Do not become disheartened or frustrated if you feel things are taking longer than you would like. Remember the alert, patient, readiness of the ever-contented Nandi. Demonstrate through your words and actions all the qualities expected of a devoted dasa throughout the application process. The best way to show sincerity is through your behavior and growth, even as you wait.

1. Read this book from cover to cover. Absorb the philosophy of Sacred Gynarchy and understand the expectations of a dasa. Take notes. If it resonates with you as truthful and good, then continue forward.

2. Determine if you feel a sincere and passionate desire to serve this specific Living Goddess. Do you think about her often? Have you dreamed about her, perhaps? Does your interest feel almost obsessive and driven from somewhere deep within you? Does your heart feel open? Do you find that you are compelled to contribute to her pleasure and ease? And do you have the time, attention, persistence, and resilience it will take to become a beloved dasa? Are you willing to work for it? Are you willing to work on yourself, maintain the protocols, and shape yourself into the best dasa you can be? If yes, move forward.

3. Take the quizzes in this section of the book and develop a good grasp of the correct answers. Answer the journal questions in each section as well and share them with the Living Goddess.

4. Begin practicing the protocols immediately, even before you are accepted. Demonstrate your willingness from the start. Be consistent and competent.

5. Fill out the application at Devidasa.org and make sure your answers to the questions are thoughtful and thorough.

6. If accepted into the church as a Sacred Gynarchist, join the online community and engage with others there. Show the Living Goddess who you are and how well you can contribute. Ask all the questions that come to mind.

7. Do an "Absolute Obedience" challenge for 108 days.

8. After having successfully completed the challenge, if you still wish to become a dasa, express your sincere heartfelt desire in a love letter to the Living Goddess. Do not be afraid to express your feelings. She will then give the gift of a special bonding hypnosis to listen to each night.

9. If you are local, offer to serve in person. If not, you may ask to arrange an in-person visit. If this is not possible, determine the best ways to serve from a distance.

10. If all goes well, when she is sure you are prepared, the Living Goddess will let you know that you have been accepted as Her dasa. You will devote your life to Her desires and needs in every way possible. You belong to Her. Your life is Hers to control. She will give you a symbolic gift to commemorate the occasion. Eventually you may be given a formal contract of service to clarify your role.

Core Concepts Quiz

This quiz tests your grasp of some of the basic concepts relevant to the role of dasa in Sacred Gynarchy.

1. Which of the following best encapsulates the relationship between the Living Goddess and the dasa as described in Sacred Gynarchy?

A) A symbolic representation of gendered power dynamics

B) A mutually negotiated partnership of equals

C) A spiritual and material relationship of consensual submission, devotion, and service

D) An abstract, transcendent spiritual ideal

2. The ultimate purpose of the Sacred Gynarchy, as articulated in the Purpose and Principles, is:

A) To create a world ruled by women gained through revolutionary upheaval, using force when necessary

B) To provide spaces where the Feminine is revered, women are safe, and consensual service to the Divine Feminine is way of life

C) To abolish all forms of organized religion

D) To enforce strict gender roles and hierarchies

3. The "Rite of Isolation" is designed to:

A) Punish the dasa for disobedience

B) Separate a dasa from the community so that he is not contaminated by worldly thoughts

C) Test the dasa's physical and psychological endurance

D) Provide a mental reset, encourage introspection, and prepare for deeper surrender

4. The Sacred Gynarchy's approach to sexual autonomy includes:

A) Women's absolute control over their bodies and sexual choices

B) Equal sexual freedom for all, regardless of gender

C) Restriction of sexual activity to procreation

D) Mandatory celibacy for men

5. The Sacred Gynarchy's stance on consent is best summarized as:

A) Authority is legitimate only with enthusiastic, informed consent

B) Consent is secondary to spiritual hierarchy

C) Consent is assumed in all relationships between women and men

D) Only women's consent matters

6. The Sacred Gynarchy's view of property and material possessions is that:

A) Accumulation of wealth is a sign of spiritual advancement and proper surrender

B) Minimalism and communal sharing are preferred; private belongings are limited

C) Each dasa should strive for personal abundance

D) Property is irrelevant to spiritual practice

7. Which of the following best describes the function of ritual pain (hormesis) in dasa practice?

A) To punish disobedience and atone for personal failings

B) To test physical strength and endurance for leadership roles

C) To trigger beneficial adaptive responses, increase resilience, and foster surrender

D) To gain social status within the Hive

8. The "Dark Feminine" is invoked in the text as:

A) A destructive force to be feared and whose malevolent tendencies can be prevented only through ritual

B) The aspect of Devi that helps identify and remove obstacles to creativity and authenticity

C) The punitive or vengeful side of the Living Goddess which must be appeased by the dasa

D) The adversary of the Divine Masculine

9. The role of the Living Goddess includes all of the following EXCEPT:

A) Embodying Devi's Desire

B) Providing a focal point for heart-opening worship

C) Maintaining transcendent perfection

D) Guiding the direction of the Hive

10. In Sacred Gynarchy, the body is viewed as:

A) An obstacle for the spirit, requiring ritual purification

B) The direct expression of spirit; body and soul are one

C) Irrational and inferior to the mind

D) A temporary vessel to be transcended

11. The practice of male chastity and orgasm denial is justified in Sacred Gynarchy primarily because:

A) It is a form of punishment for men and a way to atone for the harms of patriarchy

B) It is a requirement for all religious initiates as a kind of spiritual purification

C) It is a means of enforcing celibacy for population control, as overpopulation threatens the availability of resources

D) It prevents men from draining women's life energy, and deepens their devotion

12. The "Rite of Atonement" serves what dual purpose within the Gynarchic community?

A) To punish men for personal failings and reinforce the Hive hierarchy

B) To allow men to symbolically absorb historical harms against women and to foster empathy and humility

C) To initiate men into the Hive through physical ordeal

D) To test the dasa's obedience to arbitrary commands and ability to stretch his limits

13. Which of the following is NOT an explicit expectation of a dasa as described?

A) Anticipating the needs of the Living Goddess

B) Acting only when directly commanded

C) Offering all personal resources, including time and material wealth

D) Embracing tasks, even tedious ones, as acts of devotion

14. The analogy of Nandi, Shiva's vahana, is used to demonstrate:

A) How a dasa should perform rituals

B) The ideal of alert, patient readiness in service

C) The necessity of ritual sacrifice

D) The importance of spiritual detachment

15. How is failure interpreted within the path of the dasa?

A) As a sign of unworthiness

B) As a source of shame and guilt

C) As an opportunity for increased patience and resilience

D) As grounds for expulsion from the Hive

16. What is the ultimate purpose of the dasa's continual refinement and service?

A) To attain a final state of perfection and rest

B) To win the favor of all Living Goddesses

C) To experience ongoing spiritual blossoming until death

D) To become godlike himself

Core Concepts Answer Key:

1. C

2. B

3. D

4. A

5. A

6. B

7. C

8. B

9. C

10. B

11. D

12. B

13. B

14. B

15. C

16. C

Devidasa.org Quiz

Published at devidasa.org in 2025.

1. What is Devi primarily understood as in the Devi Doctrine?

A. The silent and absolute potential

B. The vibration of creation from which all matter, energy, thought, and movement arise

C. A goddess of war and destruction

D. A mythological figure representing the feminine

2. In the Devi Doctrine, what is considered the ultimate purpose of human life?

A. To accumulate wealth and abundance

B. To experience and enjoy Devi's endless creation

C. To pursue knowledge for its own sake

D. To transcend life and enter Siva permanently

3. What does the serpent symbolize in the Devi Doctrine?

A. Evil and temptation

B. The desire to know

C. Death and rebirth

D. The destruction of ego

4. What is the primary emotional state that negates fear, according to the Devi Doctrine?

A. Anger

B. Love

C. Desire

D. Peace

5. How is the relationship between the Divine Feminine and Divine Masculine described?

A. They are equal and oppositional forces

B. The Divine Masculine is a trellis supporting the flowering vine of the Divine Feminine

C. The Divine Feminine serves the Divine Masculine

D. They are in constant conflict, requiring balance through rituals

6. What is the role of the Living Goddess in the Devi Doctrine?

A. To embody Devi's Desire and provide a focal point for heart opening worship

B. To punish and judge devotees for their sins

C. To ensure material wealth for the community

D. To act as a symbolic figurehead with no active role

7. What is the purpose of the "isolation and embrace" rite in a Hive?

A. To punish new members for past mistakes

B. To detoxify the mind and prepare initiates for Hive life

C. To help members leave the Hive gracefully

D. To celebrate the return of the Living Goddess

8. What does the Devi Doctrine teach about reincarnation?

A. It involves the soul being reborn in a new body

B. Energy is recycled into new forms rather than the soul reincarnating

C. It does not exist in any form

D. Reincarnation is a consequence for failing to reach enlightenment

9. What is the concept of "Seva" in the Devi Doctrine?

A. A form of transactional service to gain favor from the Goddess

B. Selfless service performed without expectation of reward

C. A punishment for those who fail to follow the path

D. A ritual involving offerings to the Goddess

10. What is "Cathexis" in the Devi Doctrine?

A. A form of spiritual punishment

B. The intense focus and devotion toward the Living Goddess

C. A mantra used to connect with Devi

D. A meditation technique for self-realization

11. What are the five steps a devotee takes upon entering the service of a Living Goddess?

A. Surrender, submit, sacrifice, serve, survive

B. Meditation, devotion, sacrifice, reincarnation, enlightenment

C. Isolation, service, contemplation, enlightenment, rebirth

D. Prayer, fasting, sacrifice, knowledge, devotion

12. Which of the following best describes the concept of the "Dark Feminine"?

A. It is the destructive aspect of Devi

B. It helps identify and remove obstacles to creativity and authenticity

C. It represents the punishment for failing to love Devi

D. It opposes the Divine Masculine

13. What role does the Divine Masculine play in relation to Devi?

A. He is the counterpart who opposes Devi's desires

B. He provides structure, stability, and support to Devi's creative energy

C. He is subservient and has no significant role

D. He represents the destruction of the feminine

14. What is the ultimate goal of Bhakti (devotion) in the Devi Doctrine?

A. To eliminate ego, hatred, and fear, and replace them with bliss and wisdom

B. To attain personal enlightenment and transcend human existence

C. To reincarnate as a Living Goddess

D. To achieve material wealth and success

15. According to the Devi Doctrine, what happens after death?

A. The soul merges with Siva, or "that which is not"

B. The soul is reincarnated to continue its journey

C. The soul ascends to Devi's heavenly realm

D. The soul is judged and sent to heaven or hell

16. What is the purpose of the "Yoni Puja"?

A. To honor the masculine principle

B. To worship the source of cosmic creation and feminine energy

C. To seek forgiveness for past mistakes

D. To prepare for the afterlife

17. According to the Sacred Gynarchy, what is the primary purpose of conscious beings?

A. To worship the gods

B. To serve the Divine Masculine

C. To be Devi's sensing organs, collecting experiences

D. To attain heaven through devotion

18. How are men who crave dominance over women viewed?

A. As natural leaders

B. As protectors of society

C. As unnatural and anti-masculine

D. As misunderstood

19. What is the Sacred Gynarchy's perspective on the concept of "god" in patriarchal religions?

A. A benevolent force

B. A divisive and malicious force

C. An equal counterpart to Devi

D. A necessary evil

20. How does the Sacred Gynarchy view abortion?

A. It is strictly forbidden

B. It is treated as a sacrament

C. It is allowed only under specific circumstances

D. It is discouraged but tolerated

21. What type of organizational structure does the Sacred Gynarchy prefer?

A. Hierarchical ranking

B. Rhizomatic organization

C. Meritocracy

D. Democratic voting systems

22. What is the Sacred Gynarchy's stance on polyandry?

A. It is forbidden

B. It is normalized

C. It is discouraged

D. It is mandatory

23. How do Living Goddesses and Oracles approach conflict resolution?

A. By enforcing strict punishments

B. By exiling offenders

C. Through games and play

D. By ignoring minor conflicts

24. How does the Sacred Gynarchy view cases of sexual assault?

A. They require absolute proof before believing the victim

B. They treat it as a minor offense

C. They regard it as equal to murder

D. They forgive and reintegrate offenders

25. What does the Sacred Gynarchy teach about male chastity?

A. It is mandatory for all men

B. It is discouraged

C. It is encouraged for men who feel called to practice it

D. It has no significance in their beliefs

26. Which of the following directly serves a Living Goddess?

A. Devotee

B. Servitor

C. Oracle

D. Dasa

DeviDasa.org Quiz Answer Key:

1. B

2. B

3. B

4. B

5. B

6. A

7. B

8. B

9. B

10. B

11. A

12. B

13. B

14. A

15. A

16. B

17. C

18. C

19. B

20. B

21. B

22. B

23. C

24. C

25. C

26. D

Dasa Pop Quiz

1. You notice that a fellow dasa has left an important task or duty undone or incomplete. You:

a.) Report it immediately to the Living Goddess or Oracle. She should know he's been slacking!

b.) Confront him and tell him he must complete his task and that he is causing more work for the other dasas.

c.) Complete the task for him without complaint and say nothing.

d.) Complete the task joyfully when or if you have the time to do so and politely ask him if there was something preventing him from completing the task and if he needs help in the future.

e.) Ignore his failure to complete the task completely and let the Living Goddess deal with it when she finds out the task has not been done. It's not your responsibility and none of your business.

2. You have been given a duty, and you feel ill-equipped or too overwhelmed to take it on. You:

a.) Suck it up buttercup. You find a way to push through and do it the best you can despite being overwhelmed, confused or exhausted.

b.) Ask someone else to do it for you.

c.) Do it badly or incorrectly or complain the whole time so no one will expect you to do it again.

d.) Express your concern to the Living Goddess and ask for help or to be relieved of the duty.

e.) Hide your feelings out of embarrassment and put it off until someone else inevitably takes care of it.

3. You have been asked to do something for the Living Goddess, but it interferes with a personal plan you had made for your own pleasure. You:

a.) Immediately put your personal plan on hold or postpone it. You know your priorities: Goddess and Hive come first!

b.) Put the task off until after you have finished the activity you wanted to do for yourself. It's not an emergency.

c.) Petition the Goddess to allow you to put off the task so that you can do the thing you want to do and hope she will be understanding.

d.) Do the task and postpone your favored activity while feeling resentful and moaning about it during or after. You should have a right to do what you want!

4. You feel that your Living Goddess has been ignoring you. You:

a.) Assume she does not like or want you anymore. If she's blatantly ignoring you, she probably lost interest in you, and it might be time to take a hint and leave.

b.) Exercise patience, trusting that she will return her attention to you when it pleases her. Find other things to occupy your time and mind.

c.) Ask her why she has not been giving you any attention lately.

d.) Search your mind and observe her behavior to try to determine if you did something to upset her. Try to make amends.

e.) Ask her if there is anything you can do to serve her and make yourself indispensable by proactively doing things for her that you know she likes.

5. Your Goddess is displeased with something you have said or done. You:

a.) Accept it as valuable feedback. Apologize and ask how you might improve or make it up to her.

b.) Express shame at your own shortcomings and beg to be punished so that you never do it again.

c.) Ignore it and move on. You can't win them all. You know that her standards are impossibly high, and she's never totally pleased with you no matter what you do.

d.) Quietly retreat and self-flagellate or punish yourself for your failings. Realize that you do not deserve her and that you will always be nothing more than a useless undeserving meatsuit who is not even fit to be her doormat.

e.) Explain to her all the reasons why you failed, so she fully understands what happened, how hard you tried, and how pure and good your intentions really were.

Dasa Pop Quiz Answer Key:

1. d

2. d

3. a

4. b (e is also acceptable)

5. a

*Note the emphasis on good communication, taking responsibility, prioritizing the Living Goddess and protecting Her time and energy, and keeping your ego from acting out.

"HOW TO BEGIN" JOURNAL TOPICS

1. How do you know if you are ready to become a dasa?

2. How can you begin to discern the difference between intuition and fear/anxiety?

3. How might you embody the spirit of Nandi?

4. Write your love letter to the Living Goddess. Make it heartfelt and sincere.

GLOSSARY

CORE CONCEPTS

Explanations of some of the core concepts that a dasa must understand to function with the Sacred Gynarchy.

Gynarchy - an organization of society which centers women with men playing a supporting role. From *The Pillars of Gynarchy*: *"Gynarchy is a way of life that encompasses personal, political, and social relationships. It is the radical claim that women are natural leaders and rulers, and men can find unmatched fulfillment in supporting, serving, and pleasing them. It's based on eight pillars: Consent, Bodily Autonomy, Abundance, Collaboration, Network, the Hive, Conflict Resolution, and the Feminine as Divine."*

Devi - the Divine Feminine or Mother of All which, contrary to popular belief, has no equal opposite. The very energy that animates the whole of existence, a.k.a., Shakti. All things are energy or vibration and Devi is that vibration. She causes life to come into being from silent potential (a.k.a., Siva).

Devi is also the honorific title for a Living Goddess (e.g., Viola Devi or Devi Viola).

Living Goddess - a living embodiment of Devi who exists to be honored, revered and worshipped in order to help the worshipper quiet the ego and have the experience of heart-opening devotion. Her purpose is to receive devotion and inspire love in the heart of the dasa, and to guide the direction of a Hive and its members. There are iconic Goddesses such as those found in polytheistic religions and in myths, such as Eurynome, Inanna, Aphrodite, Durga, Kali, Hecate and others which we honor and revere within the Sacred Gynarchy. The Living Goddess, however, offers a direct and intimate connection to source in human form. She is both totally human and totally divine, and this duality is necessary for Her role.

Hive - a unique group, household, or community (in person or on-line) of people who formally practice Sacred Gynarchy and believe in the Devi Doctrine.

Dasa - sometimes translated as "slave." A member of a Hive, typically male, who worships, serves and devotes himself entirely to a particular Living Goddess and vows to put Her needs and desires above his own.

Devotee - one who is devoted, and whose life purpose is found in the service to or worship of another.

Devotion - an enthusiasm to serve, and a deep and abiding love for and loyalty to, a person, activity, or cause outside the self.

Servitor - a male servant of women (or one woman). He may or may not be a dasa or devotee.

Oracle - a female leader within Sacred Gynarchy. Usually, a member of a small group of women who collectively make decisions for a particular Hive.

Sacred Gynarchist - anyone who has joined the Devi Dasa Sacred Gynarchy to learn and find community but has not taken on an official role in a Hive or the organization itself.

Satsang - similar to a sermon, it is the sharing of knowledge in the form of writing, discussion, chant/song, or presentation by a Living Goddess.

Seva - selfless service. This is service performed in a religious context with absolutely no expectation of anything in return. No thought of reward, nor praise; no transactional thinking.

Surrender - to cease to resist. To let go of control. The ability to let go of expectations, desires, and individual will in order to experience the bliss of the desire of Devi. It is a blissful release of ego.

Ego - ego is that which allows us to have an individual sense of self. We all need some ego to remain separate and distinct and experience life from our particular and unique perspective rather than completely dissolving into oneness. However, we only need it in limited doses. When challenged, the ego becomes defensive and will fight to protect itself. The Living Goddess can help liberate you from a defensive or overactive ego.

Deconstruction - disentangling yourself from the beliefs, doctrines and covenants you were coerced or indoctrinated into in the past. Taking apart the religious ideas of your childhood or past which no longer make sense to you or feel relevant to your life.

Rhizome - the interconnected, non-hierarchical organizational structure of nature. Rhizomes are the strongest organizational structure that can exist as they are nearly indestructible. Rhizomes are made of a series of networked nodes with connections extending in all directions. Neuro-connections and the internet are both examples of Rhizomes. Ideally Gynarchy self-organizes as a Rhizome with many individual unique Hives that make up the Gynarchic network.

ADDITIONAL DEFINITIONS

Some other commonly used words defined.

Abrahamic - denoting any of the world's religions - including Judaism, Christianity, and Islam - that are said to have begun with the biblical patriarch, Abraham. Viola Devi will sometimes refer to the followers of these religions as "hammies."

Agency - the capacity of individuals to act independently and to make their own free choices.

Authority - the power or right to give orders, make decisions, and enforce obedience. Literally the author in any given situation - the one who writes the rules and decides how actions will play out.

Autonomy - the state of being self-governing. Freedom to make decisions for oneself.

Bhakti - devotion, especially of the religious type.

Chastity - refraining from sexual intercourse.

Chastity device - a device that prevents the genitals from being used for sexual intercourse.

Coercion - persuading someone to do something involuntarily, through threats or force, either blatant or subtle.

Community - a group of individuals who gather together to share in the same interests and concerns.

Compersion - the opposite of jealousy. Feeling happiness or joy because of the happiness and/or joy of another person. Feeling pleasure at witnessing another person's pleasure.

Consent - permission or explicit agreement, clearly and freely communicated without coercion.

Darshan - a Sanskrit word meaning "vision" or "appearance" or "divine sight." It is simply looking upon a deity or holy person either in person or through images. In Sacred Gynarchy it is gazing upon the image of an Iconic Goddess or Living Goddess or seeing a Living Goddess in person. Even just gazing upon the Living Goddess is an exchange of energy which serves to open the heart to deeper devotion.

Egregore - a non-physical, autonomous entity or "thought form" that arises from the collective thoughts and emotions of a group of people. These entities are believed to be "fed" by the intentions and beliefs of the group. The Abrahamic god may be an egregore.

Feminism - a social and political movement which strives for equal treatment of all humans regardless of sex or gender.

FLR - female led relationship. A romantic relationship where a woman has more authority than her partner.

Goddess - a feminine person or figure who transcends the status of mundane human either temporarily or permanently and embodies the Divine Feminine.

Ideology - a system of ideas and ideals, especially one which forms the basis of economic or political theory and policy.

Lila - divine play. We are all just Devi playing with herself, with the ultimate goal of experimenting to see what infinite varieties can be created. We are all being spontaneously created in every moment as a part of Devi's playful power.

Orgasm control - consensually giving up control over when or how one has an orgasm. Can involve teasing, denial, edging, asking permission to orgasm, or "ruined" orgasms (removing stimulation just before the point of orgasm creating a sense of frustration upon release).

Para Vidya - higher learning. Knowledge of the self and of truth.

Patriarchy - an ideology and system of social and/or political power which favors male dominance and the masculine.

Power - the capacity or ability to get what you want, or direct or influence the behavior of others or the course of events; a right or authority that is given or delegated to a person or body; physical or psychological strength; electrical energy.

Puja - a ritual of worship in which one humbles oneself in order to offer homage, reverence, and prayers to a deity. Often it involves making sensory offerings dedicated to the deity, such as flowers, incense, and sweets.

Rasa - in Sanskrit, "essence," "flavor," or "juice." It refers to the emotional flavor or delightful essence of the divine.

Real - anything that has a measurable or observable effect on material existence.

Sacrifice - to give something up which has value or importance to you.

Sadhana - a regular spiritual practice to which one commits.

Serve - to attend to someone's desires or needs.

Submissive (n.) - someone who consensually concedes authority to another, sometimes with specific conditions.

Submit - to accept or yield to the authority or will of another person.

Survive - to continue to function or prosper into the future, often against difficult odds.

Transactional - functionally based on an exchange of one thing for another thing of presumably equal value. A dasa must focus on eliminating transactional thinking.

F.A.Q.

Answers to questions from potential dasas.

Are there different levels of dasas? Like a first degree black belt, second degree, etc.?

There are no levels of dasa. It's a specific role.

sacred gynarchists = *any and all church members*

servitor = *a member who has devoted himself to serving women but who is not the personal servant of a Living Goddess (though he might be a devotee from a distance).*

dasa = *someone who has offered himself and has been accepted as a personal servant and devotee of a Living Goddess.*

For someone who has been working hard towards becoming a dasa, it seems like it would be impossible to enter dasa-hood without feeling deep love and devotion for a particular woman. Is that correct? Can someone without a woman to love, worship, and serve become a dasa... and if so, how?

Yes, it requires heartfelt devotion to a particular Living Goddess within the Devi Dasa Sacred Gynarchy. He can be a servitor with a general commitment to serving women.

It seems like a man can only become a dasa when a woman accepts him as HER dasa. His dasa position is actually defined by her acceptance of him as such. Is that a correct interpretation? That a man who doesn't have a Living Goddess to worship cannot be considered a dasa?

Yes, he must be explicitly accepted and acknowledged as such. A man who is not an accepted dasa of a Living Goddess can be a servitor, worshiping women in general, and perhaps committed to an Oracle or even a partner. Again, being a dasa is a particular role – a monk-like order within the Living Goddess's inner circle.

If a man is married and wants to serve as his wife's dasa..., can he serve his wife and still be a member of the Devi Dasa Sacred Gynarchy Church and a dasa? Or must all dasas in the church serve a Living Goddess appointed by the church?

If she is not consecrated within the church, he is considered her servitor. If she later becomes consecrated as a Living Goddess, only then would he become her dasa. If he is already partnered and wants to become a dasa to a Living Goddess, he will need the agreement of both his partner and the Living Goddess. He must not hide his dasa status from his partner. And his partner may arrange for certain boundaries in his role as dasa. It is difficult for a married man to become a dasa, but not entirely impossible with the cooperation of his wife.

Are there any men who should not aspire to becoming a dasa? In other words, is there anyone who would be automatically excluded based on age, fitness level, marital status, past history, etc.? Or is this something any man can aspire to be?

As long as he is able to carry out some duties that benefit the Living Goddess and the Hive he may be considered. Men with serious untreated mental illness or those who can't function well or contribute to the Hive would be better to remain Sacred Gynarchists. And those with a history of predatory behavior, harassment of women or any sort of sexual assault should not become dasas. We do background checks on every potential dasa.

Viola Devi is the first Living Goddess of the Devi Dasa Sacred Gynarchy. Are there currently other Living Goddesses in the Church? After reading this book, if there are 500 new Church members who all want to be dasas, will they all be dasas of the first Living Goddess, Viola Devi?

At the time of writing, Viola Devi is the only Living Goddess recognized by the church. The current timeline for Devi Dasa looks like this:

First, establish the first Mother House and Living Goddess Temple. This will be a physical place for training servitors and Oracles, as well as consecrat-

ing future Living Goddesses. It will serve as the template and prototype for future Hives.

Once established, formal training programs for servitors and dasas as well as special programs for Oracles will begin. Soon after Viola Devi will begin consecrating other Living Goddesses within the temple.

Each new Living Goddess will then establish her own Hive. Once she is operating her Hive, she may then begin consecrating new Living Goddesses, and this will continue indefinitely until a network of Hives is created.

If a man is accepted as a dasa, it would seem that a woman could change his status as a dasa at her discretion. If that were to happen through no fault of the dasa (maybe she just tires of his service or finds more devoted or inspiring dasas which she actually prefers), what happens then, especially if the dasa lives at a Hive?

This is why there is a process for acceptance. Even if more capable dasas are found, he would not be kicked out of the Hive. He would only be kicked out if he did something to hurt or anger the Living Goddess or was causing strife within the Hive (if his ego was out of control, for example). Becoming a dasa is meant to be an indefinite commitment.

It's also important to note that a dasa is also free to leave the Hive for any reason. So, the risk of abandonment is a shared one. His commitment must be genuinely desired and consensual in order to be legitimate.

Can my wife or girlfriend and I join your church together, or it is just for men at this point? Do we need any experience, religious background, etc.?

Joining the church as a Sacred Gynarchist is available to anyone of any gender, who understands and agrees with the philosophy. Like dasas, however, an Oracle or Living Goddess would go through a process to learn to fulfill their role well. And new Living Goddesses must be consecrated by a current Living Goddess to be officially recognized by the church. Living Goddess consecration is a closed practice not shared with the public.

OTHER RESOURCES

Devi Viola's Projects

GYNARCHY IO *(a collection of projects by Viola Devi)*

gynarchy.io

The Devi Dasa Sacred Gynarchy (our church)

devidasa.org

Obedient Love FLR Courses (for men and couples)

obedient.love

The Pillars of Gynarchy

pillarsofgynarchy.com

Other Important Projects

Matriarchy Times

https://www.matriarchytimes.org/

Girl At the End of the World

https://linktr.ee/daughterofumay

WHO IS DEVI VIOLA?

Viola Strepsata Voltairine has had an adventurous life, from running a BDSM dungeon in Chicago to waking up to bombs exploding while in Baghdad documenting everyday citizens during the U.S. invasion. From earning her MFA in film to writing two popular books on Gynarchy. From parenting her autistic child to leading her growing Hive in the foothills of Boulder, Colorado.

As a girl, grown men made a habit of trying to destroy their lives at young Viola's feet. Their hearts would burst open, their bodies on fire with arousal and longing, and their behavior would become obsessive and inappropriate. These adult men would literally cry with yearning to be near her. The strange, powerful effect she had on man after man was confusing. Until, at age 18, Viola Devi experienced Shaktipat while working as a museum guard looking after the relics of a Siva temple. Standing before the murtis, she describes suddenly falling into deep trances for many hours at a time and being shown a blueprint of the nature of existence. She saw the Divine Feminine as the animating life energy of all matter, and her female body, and all female bodies, as uniquely designed to hold and direct this life energy. She saw all of human history in her own DNA. She saw a field of endless knowledge and memory accessible to all. She saw that the body and spirit were not two separate ideas. She saw that there are dimensions and senses our human minds are not yet able to perceive. She began to see and understand how erotic life energy of the Divine Feminine moved in every aspect of our lives, and how literally nothing could exist without it. Coming out of these trances inside the reconstructed temple within the museum, her body was rocked with spontaneous orgasms. It would take decades for her to find words to express the knowledge gifted to her during this experience.

Having grown up without the yoke of Abrahamic religion around her neck, she decided to study all of the world's religions in college through their art and sacred texts. After earning her MFA, she dove more deeply into the study of Indian philosophy and Sanskrit via Oxford's Hindu Studies program and then Maharishi International University. She found a framework and context that helped her intellectually grasp what had happened in those profound moments in the museum. She found words in Sanskrit that fit what she needed to express. She also discovered that the wisdom of traditions like the Trika school and Shaktism came close to matching what she had experienced directly. But rather than appropriate others' traditions, she was inspired to create her own, as so many had before her. Her uniquely direct insight allowed her to become a consecrated Living Goddess.

Before founding the Devidasa Sacred Gynarchy, Viola Devi launched a private international organization called The Company, where women have their needs and desires served by a well-screened and carefully selected group of men. She has taught courses on female-led relationships for men and couples since 2018. She believes that Gynarchy begins at home, so she focused on promoting it through heterosexual romantic relationships. As she enters the second half of her life, her goal is to expand her plans from guiding personal relationships to creating a spiritual community and developing more collective experiences and spaces. Being both human and divine, Viola Devi spends her spare time reading, gardening, meditating, and creating podcasts. She is known to tell anyone who will listen that everything you need to know about life can be learned by growing a garden. She lives in Boulder with her beloved dasas. To know more about Viola Devi's philosophy, read her book *The Pillars of Gynarchy*, available wherever you like to buy books.

...and how do you pronounce it?

The phonetic pronunciation + meaning:

Devi: DEH-vee (A title meaning Goddess)

Viola: vee-OH-luh (Like the string instrument which is notoriously difficult to play.)

Stepsata: strep-SAH-tuh (It's very roughly based on the Latin word strepitus meaning "noisy," and sata the feminine Latin word for "sprung from". Alternatively, Sata is the Sanskrit for "pleasure" and is also sometimes used as one of the names of the Goddess Durga. So, in short it could roughly mean either "daughter of noise," "noisy daughter," or "pleasurable noise," "noisy pleasure" or even "noise Goddess.")

Voltairine: vol-tehr-EEN (After a woman I very much admire - the early 20th Century feminist and anarchist Voltairine DeClyre)

It's all in the name.

I went through a long process of name evolution. I did not want to keep my father's name, so I took my husband's last name, but then I left him and did not want to keep his name either. As a Gynarchist, I decided to choose an entirely new name for myself. As a result, I experienced the ecstatic rite of passage of legally claiming my self-defined identity. I would highly recommend it to any woman who has had the misfortune of growing up within the patriarchy.

I wanted to play viola as a young girl, but I was forced to learn the violin instead. And so my first name is an act of rebellion on behalf of my inner child.

Strepsata was a name that came to me out of the air while thumbing through a Latin dictionary. I wanted to find a name for my musical projects back in 2000, and I was looking for something that conveyed the idea of feminine noise. Strepsata combined both the sense of sensual flow and the staccato rhythm I craved.

Voltairine de Cleyre was an American anarchist, feminist, and writer who was considered one of the most prominent radical thinkers and activists in the late 19th and early 20th centuries. She was known for her prolific writing and powerful oratory against government authority, capitalism, and the oppression of women.

I always recommend women take the first name of a woman they admire as their surname, to create a new kind of lineage totally disconnected from male ownership and marriage. I carry on the Voltairine spirit.

But as an added bonus, she was named after Voltaire - the totally made-up pen name of a French Enlightenment writer who was a staunch advocate for civil rights like freedom of speech, freedom of religion, and the separation of church and state. He often satirized the Catholic church, though was not an atheist. So, the name has a fittingly rebellious history. There is speculation that it began with a family tradition of calling him "le petit volontaire" ("determined little thing") as a child.

On a side note: I also played around with some numerology for fun when designing my name. V is a powerful symbol of creation. In a person's name, it enhances qualities of focus, resilience, and collaboration in order to build something of meaning. People with S in their name have a magnetic presence and a deep sense of emotion. The initials VSV symbolize two strong pillars - like two downward pointing triangles that represent the divine feminine - with a magnetic emotional force vibrating, or perhaps slithering snake-like, in between them (something I feel the monogram visually conveys quite vividly!). Also, my name gives me the personality number of 7: The Number 7 in numerology is the most mystical and spiritually significant of all numbers. It represents the quest for higher truth and spiritual victory.

Shared by Viola Strepsata Voltairine, October 2025

www.ingramcontent.com/pod-product-compliance
Lightning Source LLC
Chambersburg PA
CBHW060415130626
46555CB00005B/2078